A4

English G 21

Klassenarbeitstrainer

für Schülerinnen und Schüler

mit Lösungen
Lerntipps
Kompetenztest

Vokabel Trainer
Cornelsen

Vokabeltrainer-App

Verfügbar für: iOS, Android und Windows Phone

scook

Deine **Online-Angebote** findest du hier:

1. Melde dich auf scook.de an.
2. Gib den unten stehenden Zugangscode in die Box ein.
3. Hab viel Spaß mit den Online-Angeboten.

Dein Zugangscode auf
www.scook.de

Die Online-Angebote können dort nach Bestätigung der AGB und Lizenzbedingungen genutzt werden.

wyucu-vvjmd

Cornelsen

English G 21 • Band A 4

Klassenarbeitstrainer mit Lösungen, Lerntipps und Kompetenztest

Konzeption
Dr. Ursula Mulla und Nogi Mulla, Germering

Erarbeitet von
Senta Friedrich, Tamm, Timo Keller, Kornwestheim, Bärbel Schweitzer M.A., Staufen

In Zusammenarbeit mit der Englischredaktion
Dr. Christiane Kallenbach (Projektleitung)
Jenny Dames, Lorraine Poulter (verantwortliche Redakteurinnen), Gwendolyn Düwel
Susanne Bennetreu, Stefanie Juhnke (Bildredaktion)
sowie Sarah Silver

Beratende Mitwirkung
Katrin Häntzschel, Wiesa

Tonaufnahmen
Clarity Studio Berlin (Track 1–17); The Soundhouse Ltd, London (Track 18)

Illustrationen
Dr. Volkhard Binder, Berlin (S. 34); Carlos Borrell, Berlin (S. 37 re. oben);
Constanze Schargan, Berlin (S. 11; 26; 30; 37 li. oben; 40; 43 (u. Lösungsheft S. 29); 53; 65; 70)

Bildquellen
Alamy, Abingdon (S. 4 Mitte: les polders; S. 13 Bild 4: Blend Images, Bild 7: G. H. Steele; S. 14 oben: Peter Scholey; S. 27 re.: Tom Mackie, li.: Philip Scalia; S. 28: deborah thompson; S. 29 li: Specimen, 2. v. li.: Ilene MacDonald, 2. v. re.: Travstock, re.: Aflo Foto Agency; S. 31: Megapress; S. 48: Spencer Grant; S. 72 li. Mitte: Photofusion Picture Library; S. 74 oben: Mirrorpix/Trinity Mirror; S. 75 oben: Alex Segre; S. 77: Mirrorpix/Trinity Mirror); **Art Explosion** (S. 68–69); **Caro**, Berlin (S. 37 Bild E: Riedmiller); **Corbis**, Düsseldorf (S. 18: Reuters/BRENDAN MCDERMID; S. 37 Bild A: Kevin Burke (RF); S. 51: Bettmann; S. 63 unten: Bob Krist; S. 72 re. unten: Thomas Schweizer); **Getty Images**, München (S. 62 Panoramic images (RF); S. 63 oben: Getty Images; S. 75 unten: : Lester Lefkowitz); **Grand Canyon National Park** (S. 5: NPS Photo); **Randall Hyman**, St. Louis (S. 55); **iStock**, Calgary (S. 4 2. v. li.: Marko Cadez; S. 12: Mlenny; S. 13 Bild 2: quavondo, Bild 5: Emanuele Osimo, Bild 6: Jan Paul Schrage; S. 14 unten: dra_schwartz; S. 20 Bild 2: Triggerphoto; S. 23: Winston Davidian; S. 37 Bild B: Kevin Klöpper, Bild D: J Morgan; S. 42: Sophia Tsibikaki; S. 45: kickers; S. 47: robert van beets; S. 54 oben: andrea laurita; S. 56 unten: Chris Schmidt; S. 59: Kim Gunkel; S. 66: Pali Rao; S. 71: tomograf; S. 72 re. Mitte: Steve Cole); **New England Aquarium** (S. 32); **Picture Desk**, London (S. 79 re. oben: The Kobal Collection/Warner Bros. Pictures, li. oben: The Kobal Collection/Illumination Entertainment, li. unten: The Kobal Collection/Olive Bridge Entertainment, re. unten: The Kobal Collection/Twentieth Century-Fox Film Corporation); **SADD, Inc.**, Marlborough (S. 56 Logo: Reprinted with permission from SADD, Inc.); **Shutterstock**, New York (S. 4 re: Manamana, 2. v. re.: Coburn, li.: Samuel Acosta; S. 6: Anton Foltin; S. 8 Bild 1: auremar, Bild 2: Monkey Business Images, Bild 3: AVAVA, Bild 4: Monkey Business Images, Bild 5: Dolly; S. 13 Bild 1: Iwona Grodzka, Bild 3: Worldpics, Bild 8: ronfromyork, Bild 9: Simone van den Berg, Bild 10: jcpjr; S. 16: Jose Gil; S. 20 Bild 1: Elena Elisseeva, Bild 3: Catalin Petolea, Bild 4: paulaphoto, Bild 5: Yuri Arcurs, Bild 6: Jacek Chabraszewski, Bild 7: Gelpi, Bild 8: RoxyFer; S. 36: jeff Metzger; S. 37 Bild C: tororo reaction, Bild F: Andresr; S. 54 Hintergrund: RTimages; S. 61: Khirman Vladimir; S. 72 re. oben: Monkey Business Images, li. unten: Goodluz; S. 74 re. unten: wavebreakmedia ltd, li. unten: Voronin76, Mitte: Monkey Business Images)

Textquellen
S. 5 *Become a Junior Ranger!* adapted from "Be a Junior Ranger" (http://www.nps.gov/grca/forkids/beajuniorranger.htm) (05.01.2011), © Grand Canyon National Park; S. 21 *The Empire State Building* adapted and abridged from http://www.esbnyc.com/observatory.asp (05.01.2011), © Empire State Building Company L.L.C.; S. 24 The Boston Freedom Trail® adapted from www.thefreedomtrail.org (17.01.2011) © Freedom Trail Foundation®.

Titelbild
Constanze Schargan, Berlin; Corel Library (US Flag Hintergrund)

Layout und technische Umsetzung
Heike Freund, Hameln

Umschlaggestaltung
Klein & Halm Grafikdesign, Berlin

www.cornelsen.de
www.EnglishG.de

1. Auflage, 8. Druck 2017

Druck: H. Heenemann, Berlin

ISBN 978-3-06-032250-3

INHALT

ACHTUNG, KLASSENARBEIT!

Liebe Schülerin, lieber Schüler,
wer sich gut vorbereitet, kann der nächsten Klassenarbeit gelassen entgegen blicken. Der Klassenarbeitstrainer unterstützt dich ganz gezielt beim Üben für alle Klassenarbeiten. Du findest zu jeder Unit zwei Klassenarbeiten, mit denen du alle Fertigkeiten (skills) trainieren kannst, die du für die Klassenarbeiten benötigst.

Einige Tipps für ein erfolgreiches Lernen mit deinem Klassenarbeitstrainer:

Vorbereitung
Informiere dich genau über die kommende Klassenarbeit, damit du weißt, was dran kommt. In einem Lernplan legst du fest, welche Aufgaben du an welchem Tag bearbeiten willst. Plane dazu genügend Zeit ein. Hole dir bei Unklarheiten Hilfe.
Am Tag vor der Arbeit wiederholst du nur kurz.

Lernheft
Führe ein Schreibheft für die Schreibaufgaben und zusätzlichen Übungen. Achte auf Übersichtlichkeit (Datum, Überschrift, Aufgabe, Seite). Lege auf der 1. Seite ein Inhaltsverzeichnis an. So kannst du bei Unklarheiten immer wieder nachschlagen. Es hilft dir auch, wenn du eine Aufgabe wiederholen möchtest.

Lösungen und Punkteschlüssel
Du findest die Lösungen zusammen mit deinen Audios unter www.scook.de. Dort kannst du sie dir mit deinem Code freischalten. Dein Code steht am Anfang des Hefts auf der ersten Seite. Vergleiche deine Lösungen mit den möglichen Lösungen. Sieh dir dabei deine Fehler ganz genau an und überlege, was du falsch gemacht hast. Nur so kannst du daraus lernen und die Fehler in Zukunft vermeiden.
In den Lösungen findest du auch die Hörtexte und Lerntipps mit Verweisen zu weiteren Übungen.
Der Punkteschlüssel hilft dir, deine Leistung einzuschätzen.

Kompetenztest
Am Ende des Heftes findest du einen Kompetenztest, mit dem du dich auf eine zentrale Leistungsüberprüfung (auch: „Vergleichsarbeit", „Vera 8", „Diagnosearbeit", „Lernstandserhebung") vorbereiten kannst.
Dieser Kompetenztest steht nicht in Zusammenhang mit einer bestimmten Unit im Buch.

Übrigens: Die Klassenarbeiten in diesem Heft prüfen das Gelernte sehr ausführlich ab.
Du brauchst daher für die Bearbeitung länger als eine Schulstunde. Natürlich kannst du dir die Klassenarbeiten auch auf einzelne Tage aufteilen oder bestimmte Aufgaben ganz gezielt üben.

Let's get started!

Ich wünsche dir viel Freude und vor allem viel Erfolg beim Üben und Lernen mit deinem Klassenarbeitstrainer.

Have fun with English!

Bärbel Schweitzer

Introduction

Gesamtpunktzahl ____/74	Note ____

READING

____/11

Become a Junior Ranger![1]

What is a Junior Ranger?

Junior Rangers are good friends of the Grand Canyon National Park. They learn about the Grand Canyon, have fun and tell their friends, families and classmates back home about the Grand Canyon. Junior Rangers know a lot about the park, so they can give information about it to others. They also help to protect[2] the park and make sure that it stays as wonderful as it is today.

How can you become a Junior Ranger?

At the Grand Canyon, there are different ways of becoming a Junior Ranger. All of our Junior Ranger programs are free.

To become a Junior Ranger, pick up the Junior Ranger Activity Booklet at the Visitor Center at the Grand Canyon View Information Plaza. Then do the activities you find in the booklet for your age group. There are different activities to do: for example you have to write about the park and answer questions on it. You also have to write poems and visit one of the Rangers' daily programs.
There are three different types of Junior Rangers for children aged 4+:

Ages 4–7: Raven

Ages 8–10: Coyote

Ages 11+: Scorpion

When you finish your activities, bring the booklet back to the Visitor Center and show it to a Ranger. Each Junior Ranger will get a Grand Canyon Junior Ranger certificate[3] and patch[4].

Phantom Rattler Junior Ranger (ages 4–14)

This is a very special program because only kids who hike or ride the mules down to the bottom of the Grand Canyon to Phantom Ranch can become Phantom Rattler Junior Rangers! There are two jobs you must do to become a Phantom Rattler Junior Ranger: first, you have to make it to Phantom Ranch, and second, you have to do the activities in the Junior Ranger booklet. If you do both, you will get your patch, a certificate and a baseball cap from a Ranger at Phantom Ranch.

[1] Junior Ranger ['dʒuːniə(r) 'reɪndʒə(r)] *jugendlicher „Park Ranger"* [2] (to) protect [prə'tekt] *schützen*
[3] certificate [sə'tɪfɪkət] *Urkunde* [4] patch [pætʃ] *Aufnäher, Abzeichen (aus Stoff)*

1 About the text

_____/2

Read the text. What are the two main ideas in the text? Write two sentences.

____

____

2 Junior Rangers and the Grand Canyon

_____/9

Tick (✔) the correct box. Be careful: sometimes more than one answer is correct.

1 Junior Rangers ...	a) learn a lot of information about the Grand Canyon.	
	b) get money for their job.	
	c) help to look after the park.	
2 If you want to become a Junior Ranger, ...	a) you have to pay to take part in the programme.	
	b) you have to do lots of activities.	
	c) you have to read books about the Grand Canyon.	
3 At the Visitor Center ...	a) you can get the Junior Ranger Activity Booklet.	
	b) you can show your poem to a Ranger.	
	c) you can visit Phantom Ranch.	
4 Children aged nine ...	a) can become Scorpion Junior Rangers.	
	b) are too old to become Raven Junior Rangers.	
	c) can become Phantom Rattler Junior Rangers.	
5 All Phantom Rattler Junior Rangers ...	a) have been on a boat trip on the Colorado river.	
	b) get a baseball cap and a certificate.	
	c) work at the Grand Canyon View Information Plaza.	
6 Phantom Ranch ...	a) is only for Coyote and Scorpion Rangers.	
	b) is at the bottom of the Grand Canyon.	
	c) is a place you can get to by riding a mule.	

LANGUAGE

_____ / 39

1 WORDS An alphabetical list

_____ / 13

a) *The letters of the new words are mixed up. Put them in the correct order and write the words into the list. (9P)*

A	ewemoas	N	eaivtN nrmAacie
B	uicablsonr	O	
C	tcolieclon	P	repfre
D	nuiaosrd	Q	
E	apisycllee	R	ftar
F	lniylfa	S	ttrihsag
G	ogger	T	olto
H	whghyai	U	milaettu
I	nicodiifanitte	V	
J		W	
K	otlmeiekr	X	
L	yerla	Y	
M	eulm	Z	

b) *Write four sentences with words from **a)**. (4P)*

1 ______________________________

2 ______________________________

3 ______________________________

4 ______________________________

2 Getting by in English

_____ / 4

Write what you would say in English.

Was sagst du, …

1 wenn du keine Ahnung hast, was du heute Abend anziehen sollst?

____

2 wenn du nicht weißt, wo du deine Fahrkarte kaufen sollst?

____

3 wenn du keine Ahnung hast, wie du die Geschichte erzählen sollst?

____

4 wenn du fragen willst, wie du zum nächsten Supermarkt kommst?

____

3 GRAMMAR Talking about national parks

_____ /6

These people are talking about national parks. Complete the sentences.
*Use the **simple past** or the **present perfect**.*

1 

I ________________________ (go) to the Grand Canyon with my family last summer.

2 

The baby ________________________ (not hike) in the Grand Canyon yet.

3 

Last week I ________________________ (give) a presentation on national parks in the US.

4 

I ________________________ (not have) time yesterday to tell you about my trip to Death Valley.

5 

We ________________________ (visit) many national parks on our last two vacations, but we ________________________ ________________________ (never be) to the Grand Canyon.

Simple past oder present perfect?

	Wann?	Signalwörter	Beispiel (positiv)	Beispiel (negativ)
Simple past	• Vergangenes • genauer Zeitpunkt	last weekend/ month/year yesterday a week/month/ day ago in 2007	I **went** to the Grand Canyon last weekend.	We **didn't go** to the Grand Canyon last weekend.
Present perfect	• Vergangenes • Zeitpunkt unwichtig	already/just/ ever/never/yet	He **has** already **seen** a condor.	I **haven't seen** a condor yet.

4 GRAMMAR Junior Rangers on the internet

___/12

You want to know what it is like to be a Junior Ranger. On the internet you find Andy Fisher's website. He's a Junior Ranger.

You decide to ask Andy some questions. Complete the questions below and write them in your exercise book.
*Use the verbs in brackets to ask questions in the **simple present** or in the **simple past**. (7P)*

1 the Junior Ranger programme – (hear about) – how – you?
2 why – a Junior Ranger – you – (become)?
3 the programme with the Park Ranger – (be) – interesting?
4 (do) – what – a Park Ranger?
5 you – what – to become a Junior Ranger – (do)?
6 (stay) – you – in the Grand Canyon – where?
7 (become) – you – a Junior Ranger – when?

Fragebildung	
Simple present	**Simple past**
Are you a Junior Ranger?	**Was** it fun at the Grand Canyon?
Do you like the Grand Canyon?	**Did** you go to the Grand Canyon last weekend?
Does the Park Ranger know a lot about the park?	**Did** he become a Junior Ranger?
How **do** I become a Junior Ranger?	When **did** you become a Junior Ranger?

Now you

Write down five more questions you would like to ask Andy in your exercise book.
Ask at least two questions with question words. (5P)

5 GRAMMAR If I was a Junior Ranger, ...

___/4

Conditional sentences (type 1 and type 2)	
Conditional sentences (type 1)	
If-clause: **simple present**	Main clause: **will-future / modal auxiliary / imperative**
If you **make** it to Phantom Ranch,	you **will get** your patch.
If you **visit** the Grand Canyon,	you **can become** a Junior Ranger.
If you **are** a Junior Ranger,	**tell** your classmates all about the Canyon!
Conditional sentences (type 2)	
If-clause: **simple past**	Main clause: **conditional 1**
If he **was** a Junior Ranger,	he **would be** very happy.
If they **were** seven years old,	they **couldn't become** Coyotes.
If she **visited** Phantom Ranch,	she **might have** a good time.

Complete the following sentences about the Junior Ranger programme with the correct form of the verb in brackets.

1 If you ______________ (be) nine years old, you can join the Coyote Junior Rangers.

2 Tom ______________ (have) a lot of fun if he was at Phantom Ranch.

3 If you do all the activities in the booklet, you ______________ (become) a Junior Ranger.

4 If the Ranger ______________ (like) your poem, she'll smile.

WRITING

____/ 24

An article about the Grand Canyon

Last summer you visited the Grand Canyon with your family.
Write an article about this trip for the English language part of your school magazine.

a) *First look at the mind map and complete it with your own ideas and the ideas from the box. (5P)*

> **Texte schreiben**
>
> Achte beim Schreiben darauf,
> - deinen Text gut zu strukturieren. Die Mindmap gibt dir bereits eine Struktur für deinen Text vor.
> - deine Sätze zu verbinden (z. B. **linking words**: **too**, **because**, **but**, **so**, **and**) und auszubauen (Adjektive).
> - deinen Text zu strukturieren (**paragraphs**, **topic sentences**).
> - ein passendes Ende für deinen Text zu finden.
> - deinen Text inhaltlich und sprachlich zu überprüfen.

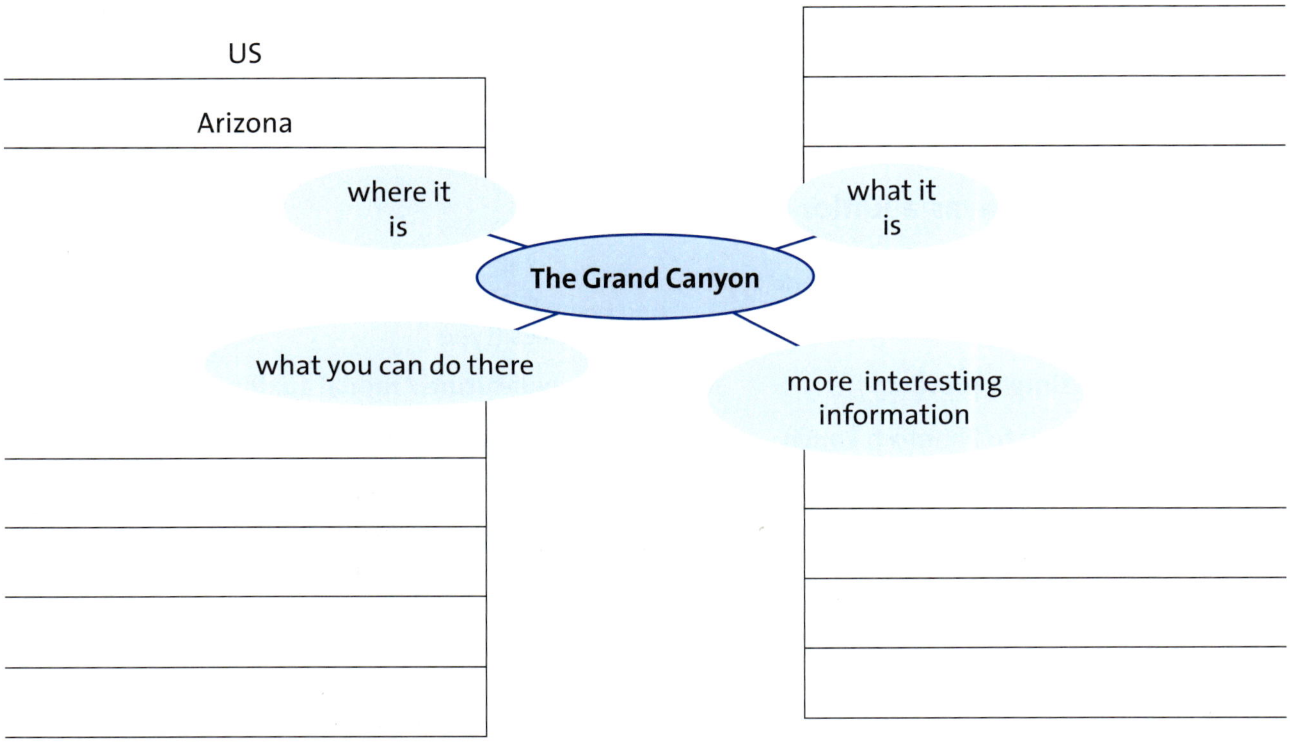

- deep gorge formed by Colorado River
- national park since 1919
- 5 million visitors every year
- mule trips
- visit skywalk (good view)
- stay in the park overnight
- walk into the canyon on trails
- walls of multi-coloured rocks
- Park Rangers look after park
- go rafting

b) *Then write a text of about 120–180 words. (19P)*
You can start your article like this:

The Grand Canyon

The Grand Canyon in Arizona is one of the most famous national parks in the US. The Canyon …

Gesamtpunktzahl ______ /57	Note ______

LISTENING

______ /12

01 Big Apple Radio

You are on holiday in New York and are listening to Big Apple Radio.

> Versuche beim ersten Hören zunächst ganz allgemein zu verstehen, worum es in dieser Sendung geht. Vor dem Hören solltest du die erste Aufgabe lesen.

1 Subway stories

______ /3

Look at the pictures. Then listen to the radio programme. What are the people talking about? Tick (✔) the three correct pictures. Be careful: there are more pictures than you need.

A

B

C

D

E

F

2 About the radio programme

___/9

Read the following sentences. Then listen to the text again and tick (✔) the correct box.

1 The presenter of the radio programme ...	a) works at night.	
	b) asks people to call her.	
	c) tells her own story about the subway.	
2 Cindy's story happened ...	a) last summer.	
	b) last spring.	
	c) a month ago.	
3 Cindy was on the subway ...	a) on her way to the zoo.	
	b) on the way home from work.	
	c) on her way to see her friend.	
4 Cindy ...	a) left her present on the subway.	
	b) met a young woman on the subway.	
	c) took the wrong subway.	
5 Sam ...	a) has never been on the subway before.	
	b) has got a twelve-year-old sister.	
	c) is twelve years old.	
6 Sam ...	a) went on the subway with her brother.	
	b) took the subway to Manhattan.	
	c) went on the subway on a school trip.	
7 Sam ...	a) helped an old woman on the subway.	
	b) couldn't pay for her subway ticket.	
	c) went with her brother to the wrong station.	
8 Ana-María ...	a) has had problems finding the right station.	
	b) always feels very hot on the subway.	
	c) is spending her holidays in New York.	
9 Ana-María ...	a) has met lots of nice people on the subway.	
	b) lost her subway map.	
	c) doesn't like using the subway.	

LANGUAGE

____ / 25

1 WORDS In the city

____ / 10

Look at the pictures. Then find the correct words and complete the sentences.
Be careful: sometimes you have to find the correct form of the word too.

> **Die richtige Form finden**
>
> Notwendige Veränderungen können sein:
> - bei **Nomen**: Pluralform
> - bei **Verben**: die richtige Zeitform, z. B. **simple present** oder **simple past** (to walk: he walk**s** ▸ he walk**ed**)

1 Cars must stop at ______________________.

2 Let's pay at the ______________________ over there.

3 Don't ______________________. Keep the city clean.

4 At the ______________________ you can order our delicious bagels.

5 Harry and Sally are kissing on the ______________________.

6 If you park here, you have to pay a ______________________.

7 ______________________ was very poor. It was almost impossible to see the Statue of Liberty.

8 In an ______________________ you must call 911.

9 "Mmm, this bagel ______________________ great. Would you like to try one too?"

10 There's a ______________________ at our church every Sunday.

2 GRAMMAR Life in the city

____/15

Some friends are talking about their lives in New York.
*Complete what they say. Use **gerunds** of the verbs in the box. (10P)*

help • live • look • ride • shop • take • taste • travel • visit • walk

The Guggenheim Museum

1 I like ____________ at all the cool buildings here.

2 I love ____________ the museums.

3 My sister and I don't like ____________ by subway.

4 ____________ a bike can be dangerous in Manhattan.

5 I dream of ____________ in Brooklyn some day.

6 ____________ is great in New York. Here you can shop till you drop!

7 The policeman[1] is tired of ____________ tourists when they are lost.

8 Most tourists enjoy ____________ around Manhattan.

9 If you like ____________ interesting food, go to a deli in Chinatown!

10 ____________ a break in Central Park is a good idea after a long day in New York.

Now you

*Write five more sentences about living in a town or city. Use **gerunds**. (5P)*

____

____

____

____

____

[1] policeman [pə'li:smən] *Polizist*

WRITING

____ / 20

A subway story for the school magazine

You are a student at City High School, New York. You heard the radio programme with the subway stories. Now you want to write your personal story about the subway for the school magazine.

Write your story (about 100–150 words).

- Sammle zunächst Ideen (mit einer Mindmap, einer Liste oder den „fünf Ws“).
- Dein Text sollte aus drei Teilen (Einleitung, Hauptteil, Schluss) und einer passenden Überschrift bestehen.
- Überlege dir einen interessanten oder spannenden Anfang und ein passendes Ende und teile deinen Hauptteil in mindestens zwei Absätze ein.
- Schmücke deine Sätze aus durch abwechslungsreiche Wortwahl, Adjektive, Adverbien usw.
- Schreibe deinen Text in der Vergangenheit.
- Lies deinen Text durch und korrigiere eventuelle Fehler.
- Auf S. 168/169 im **Writing Course** deines Buches findest du weitere Hinweise.

Use at least four of the following phrases in your story:

a parcel • 'you've forgotten your parcel' • what could I do? • poster: call the police • name on the parcel • thank-you card • got $50

Klassenarbeit B

Gesamtpunktzahl ohne Speaking ______ / 68 Note ______
Gesamtpunktzahl mit Speaking ______ / 94 Note ______

READING

____ / 22

The Empire State Building Run-Up

Sieh dir vor dem Lesen des Textes Aufgabe 1 an. Überfliege dann den Lesetext. Auf diese Weise bist du schnell dazu in der Lage, die erste Aufgabe zu lösen.

1 Over three million people visit the skyscraper each year to enjoy the fantastic views of New York City from the 86th and the 102nd floor observatories. Every year the building also holds a running event called the Empire State Building Run-Up. It's a race[1] where runners run up 1,576 steps to the 86th floor Observatory.

2 The first Empire State Building Run-Up was in 1978 and was the idea of Fred Lebow, President of the New York Road Runners Club. It was part of a project to get more people interested in running. The Empire State Building Run-Up is the most well-known and also the oldest stair race[2]. It's not the only stair race in the world. Other stair races take place in tall buildings across the US, Europe and Asia.

3 Each year about 500 people would like to run in the race but there are only 300 places. You have to apply[3] in writing. The New York Runners Club then chooses the runners for the race. Although it is not a long-distance[4] race, it is a hard race. Runners have to be really fit and give everything to get to the top.

4 The runners come from all over the world. In 2009 a 24-year-old student from Stuttgart, Germany won the race with a time of 10 minutes and 7 seconds. He won the race for the fourth time. A 35-year-old Australian woman living in Singapore won the women's race in 13 minutes and 27 seconds. Her win was quite amazing. Early in the race somebody pushed her to the side. She fell and hurt her left knee and her face. At that time she was about 20th in the race, and the leaders were some floors higher up. It's very difficult to run past other runners while they are running, but the Australian woman was able to do it although her leg hurt. In the end she was the winner. She ended up winning the race by 13 seconds.

[1] race [reɪs] *hier: Laufwettkampf* [2] stair race ['steə(r) reɪs] *Treppenlauf*
[3] (to) apply [ə'plaɪ] *sich bewerben* [4] long-distance [ˌlɒŋ 'dɪstəns] *Langstrecken-*

1 What is the article about?

____/1

Explain what the Empire State Building Run-Up is in one sentence using your own words.

____

____

2 Missing headings

____/4

Match the headings to the paragraphs 1–4.
Be careful: there are two more headings than you need.

A The winners
B High up
C Safety
D How to take part
E Prizes
F History

1		2		3		4	

3 About the run

____/8

Match the sentence halves and draw lines to complete the sentences about the article.
Be careful: there are more endings than you need. (5P)

1 The Empire State Building Run-Up
2 People who would like to run
3 The Run-Up was the idea of
4 About 500 runners
5 It is a hard race, so

a) want to be in the race.
b) and a women's race.
c) is a long-distance race.
d) runners must be really fit.
e) takes place every year.
f) the president of the New York Road Runners Club.
g) four times.
h) have to write a letter to the New York Road Runners Club.

Now you

Complete the following phrases with information from the text. (3P)

1 Fred Lebow wanted more people ______________________.

2 Not everyone can ______________________.

3 A student has won ______________________.

4 Questions about the run

___/9

Mary from San Diego is interested in the race and has a lot of questions.
She reads the article about the Empire State Building Run-Up and finds answers to seven of her questions.
Tick (✔) the seven questions. (7P)

1 When is the next race?	
2 How many floors do runners run up?	
3 When was the first race?	
4 What are the prizes for the winners?	
5 How do the runners train for the race?	
6 Are there stair races in other parts of the world?	
7 How many people run?	
8 How old do you have to be to take part in the race?	
9 Are runners from New York only?	
10 Is there a women's race?	
11 Can I watch the race?	
12 Have there been any accidents?	

The winner in 2009

Now you

Write two more questions the text answers. (2P)

____

____

LANGUAGE

___/31

1 WORDS American and British English

___/12

a) *Collect six words that are **different** in American and British English.*
Write them into the table. (6P)

American English	British English
apartment	flat

b) *Write six words with a* ***different spelling*** *in American and British English into the table. (6P)*

American English	British English
center	centre

2 GRAMMAR After the fire

____/9

Complete the following dialogue between two firefighters, one from Manhattan and one from the Bronx. Fill in reflexive pronouns (e.g. ***himself****).*

Bill Did you hear about the terrible fire yesterday?

Ian Yes, I was there ________________. An old factory was on fire.

Bill Was anybody hurt?

Ian The fire ________________ didn't hurt anybody because the building was empty at the time, but we had to stop pedestrians from getting too close so they wouldn't hurt ________________. One woman wanted to get through because she said she had seen her cat run into the building before the fire broke out.

Bill Were you and the other firefighters in danger?

Ian Not really, but at one point we had to save ________________ and hide behind a fire truck[1] because a ladder collapsed.

Bill Wow, that sounds exciting. Did you hurt ________________ at all?

Ian You won't believe it, but I hurt ________________ a little when I fell over on the sidewalk because I wasn't looking where I was going! And one of our men hurt ________________ when a stone fell on his shoulder.

Bill I really didn't know you were there. I heard about the fire on the news. There was a journalist who'd seen the fire and the rescue operation ________________. He spoke about it in a very dramatic way.

Ian Yes, my team heard that report too. It's always strange to hear about something like that if you have put out the fire ________________.

[1] fire truck ['faə(r) trʌk] *(AE) Feuerwehrauto*

3 GRAMMAR About New York

____ / 10

These teenagers are talking about New York. First read what they say. Then complete the sentences about them. Use the verb phrase in brackets and choose the correct verb from the box to form the ***gerund****. (7P)*

go • have • leave • move • travel • wait • watch • write

1

Sue
"I would like to see a famous Broadway show."

2

Mike
"I don't like waiting for the subway in the morning."

3

Alice
"I have to take the train to New York every day."

4

Mark
"I don't want to leave my car in the Bronx. It might be stolen."

5

Elias
"I'm the greatest writer of speeches in the world!"

6

Jennifer
"I would never want to move away from New York."

7

Sophie
"Every lunchtime I go for a walk in Central Park."

8

Alan
"I'd rather have a picnic than go cycling."

1 Sue dreams of watching a famous Broadway show. (dream of)

2 Mike ______________________________ (hate)

3 Alice ______________________________ (be tired of)

4 Mark ______________________________ (be afraid of)

5 Elias ______________________________ (be good at)

6 Jennifer ______________________________ (can't imagine)

7 Sophie ______________________________ (like)

8 Alan ______________________________ (prefer)

Now you

What do you think about living in your town? Write three more sentences in your exercise book. You can use the same verbs again. (3P)

MEDIATION

____/15

Visiting New York City

The Empire State Building

86th Floor Observatory:

The 86th Floor Observatory, 1,050 feet (320 meters), reached by high-speed, automatic elevators. Has two areas: a glass-enclosed area, which is heated in winter and cooled in summer, and a large outdoor area on all four sides of the building. There are high-powered binoculars in the outdoor area which visitors can use at a minimal cost. Of course, disabled visitors are welcome.

102nd Floor Observatory:

102nd Floor Observatory tickets are only sold upon arrival at the Empire State Building at a cost of $15.00 in addition to regular admission tickets.

Observatory Hours:

Open daily, 365 days a year.
8.00 am to 2.00 am 7 days a week. Last elevators go up at 1.15 am.

IMPORTANT: Everyone must go through the security check when entering the building. No glass or bottles are permitted in the Observatory. Cameras and camcorders are allowed but no tripods. Please view our Security and Visitor Information for more details.

Admission Prices at the Building:	
Empire State Building Express Pass	$45
Adults (13–61)	$20
Children (6–12)	$14
Seniors (62+)	$18
Military in uniform	Free
Children (5 or younger – with adult)	Free

ESB Express Pass:

The lines at the Empire State Building Observatory are as well-known as the building itself. There are three different lines. The first one is the security line that everyone must go through. Next comes the ticket line. Visitors who already have tickets need not wait in this line, which can save quite a lot of time when we are busy. The third and last line is for the elevators that take you to the Observatory.

Some people have said that it doesn't matter how long you have to wait – the view from the Empire State Building is too awesome to miss. Other people have said they couldn't visit the Empire State Building Observatory because they just didn't have enough time to see and do everything while in New York City. Now you can. By buying an Express Pass you can always go to the front of each of the three lines.

Need more time for shopping or seeing a show? Perhaps there's a restaurant that you just have to experience? The Express Pass is the answer for you. It gives you enough time to do it all in the city that never sleeps.

☞ Versuche Wörter, die du nicht oder nicht mehr weißt, aus dem Zusammenhang zu erschließen.

Ein Freund deiner Familie möchte nach New York fahren. Während seines Aufenthalts will er ins Empire State Building. Er war auf dessen Website, aber da sein Englisch nicht so gut ist, bittet er dich, ihm die wichtigsten Informationen zu den folgenden Themen mitzuteilen:

1 Informationen über die Aussichtsplattform im 86. Stockwerk *(mindestens fünf Hinweise)* (5P)

____

____

____

____

____

2 Informationen über die Eintrittskarten für die Aussichtsplattform im 102. Stockwerk (wo man sie bekommt, wie viel sie kosten) (2P)

____

____

3 Öffnungszeiten der Aussichtsplattformen (Abendöffnungszeit: wie lange, was gibt es zu beachten?) (3P)

____

____

____

4 Informationen über den Empire State Building Express Pass (Preis und der Vorteil des Passes) (4P)

____

____

5 Gibt es einen Vorteil, wenn man bereits eine Eintrittskarte hat? (1P)

____

SPEAKING

_____ / 26

02 A street interview

Every year millions of people visit New York. To find out what they like and don't like about the city, the New York Tourist Organization asks people to take part in street interviews.

Listen to an interview with a Spanish visitor.

☞ Höre dir das Interview an und notiere die Formulierungen, die hilfreich sein könnten, wenn du im **Now you** selbst an einem Interview teilnimmst.

Now you

a) *You are visiting New York and are taking part in a street interview. Here are a few questions to prepare for the interview. Make notes. (6P)*

Where are you from? ______________________________

How old are you? ______________________________

Why are you in New York? ______________________________

Where are you staying? / How long for? ______________________________

Are you in a group? Or alone? ______________________________

How long have you been in New York? ______________________________

What have you seen already? ______________________________

What else would you like to do here? ______________________________

What kind of transportation[1] have you used? ______________________________

What do you like about New York? ______________________________

What don't you like? ______________________________

Will you come again? Why? ______________________________

03 ***b)*** *Now listen to the questions. Stop the recording when you hear the beep. Continue listening when you have said your part. (20P)*

[1] transportation (AE) [ˌtrænspɔːˈteɪʃn] *Verkehrsmittel*

Klassenarbeit A

Gesamtpunktzahl ohne Speaking ______ / 87	Note ______
Gesamtpunktzahl mit Speaking ______ / 113	Note ______

READING

______ / 20

The Boston Freedom[1] Trail®

Welcome to the Freedom Trail!

Visitors to Boston, welcome to the Freedom Trail. There is no other place in the United States where you can better explore the rich history of America's Revolution – the events that led up to the historic break from Britain and the brave people who took part in them.

The Freedom Trail is a 2.5-mile walking trail that leads you to 16 nationally important historic places. The Freedom Trail today is a unique collection of museums, churches, meeting houses, parks and a ship that tell the story of the American Revolution.

Boston Latin School – The oldest public school

Founded on April 13, 1635, Boston Latin is America's oldest public school. On School Street a statue of ex-student Benjamin Franklin marks the location of the old Boston Latin schoolhouse. Four of the men who signed the Declaration of Independence[2] were students at Boston Latin: Franklin, Adams, Hancock and Paine. But of the four, only three graduated: Benjamin Franklin, though one of America's greatest minds, is also one of its most famous high school dropouts[3].

The school has continued in different locations until today and, unlike in the days of the Revolution, these days the students are both boys and girls.

Old South Meeting House

Built in 1729 as a Puritan meeting house, Old South Meeting House was the stage for some of the most dramatic events leading up to the American Revolution. The most important was a meeting that happened in December 1773. Over 30 tons of tea from Britain sat on board three ships in Boston Harbour. Not wanting to pay tax[4] on the tea to the British, thousands of Bostonians crowded into Old South Meeting House to take part in a discussion of what should be done with the tea. After they finally realized that the tea couldn't be sent back to England, men dressed as Mohawk Indians walked to Griffin's Wharf where the tea was destroyed. This event became known as the Boston Tea Party.

Old State House

The Old State House was the official building of the British Government[5] before the Revolution. In 1776 the Declaration of Independence was read out from here.

Some of the most important events leading up to the Revolution took place inside and around this Georgian house. Here, Samuel Adams said that taxation without representation was unfair. Outside its doors the Boston Massacre took place in 1770, leading to the deaths of five men and increasing public opposition to the British Government.

[1] freedom ['fri:dəm] *Freiheit* [2] Declaration of Independence [ˌdekləˈreɪʃn, ɪndiˈpendəns] *Unabhängigkeitserklärung*
[3] dropout ['drɒpaʊt] *Schulabbrecher* [4] tax [tæks] *Steuer* [5] government ['gʌvənmənt] *Regierung*

1 Which mind map is it?

___ / 4

a) *Read the text and decide which of the mind maps fits the text. (1P)*

1

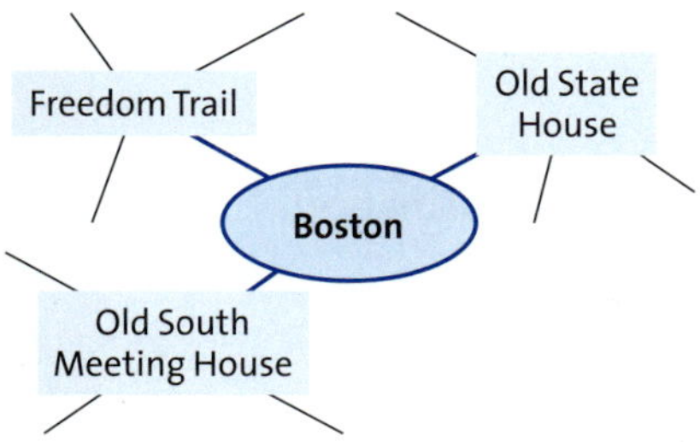

2

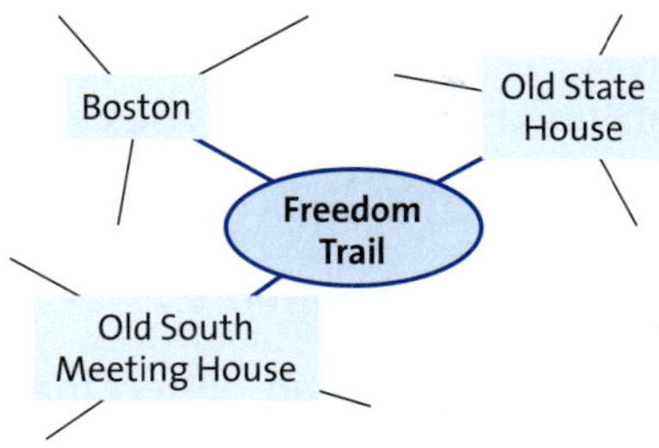

3

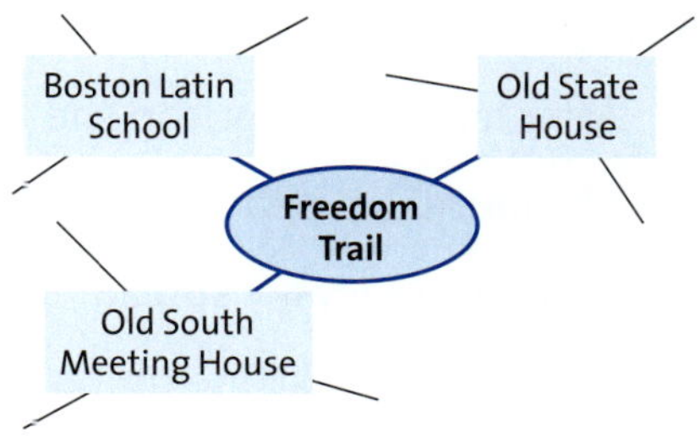

b) *Now copy the correct mind map into your exercise book and add the words from the box. Be careful: three lines have to stay empty. (3P)*

Boston Massacre • Boston Tea Party • British Government • Declaration of Independence • discussion • Statue of Benjamin Franklin

2 More about the Freedom Trail

___ / 16

Read the text again and decide if the statements are right, wrong or not in the text.

		Right	Wrong	Not in the text
1 The Boston Freedom Trail	a) This is a museum about the American Revolution.			
	b) It gives information on different places in Boston.			
	c) It has been designed for cars.			
	d) It helps people to understand why and how the USA became independent from Britain.			
2 Boston Latin School	a) Benjamin Franklin's statue is the oldest in Boston.			
	b) Four of the men who signed the Declaration of Independence went to Boston Latin School.			
	c) Benjamin Franklin was a good student.			
	d) Boston Latin School still exists today.			
3 Old South Meeting House	a) In 1729, a discussion about taxes on tea took place at the meeting house.			
	b) Twenty Bostonians dressed as Indians.			
	c) A meeting which led to the Boston Tea Party took place at the Meeting House.			
	d) Old South Meeting House was full of tea in 1773.			
4 The Old State House	a) The Old State House was where the British Government worked after 1776.			
	b) The Declaration of Independence was written in the Old State House.			
	c) Samuel Adams was against taxation without representation.			
	d) The Boston Massacre started in the Old State House in 1772.			

LANGUAGE

____ / 50

1 WORDS Find the correct words.

____ / 8

Read the following sentences and underline the correct words.

1 After ten years in prison she was **pardoned** / **sentenced** / **chased**.
2 The journalist didn't want to talk about the **handout** / **routine** / **source** of his information.
3 The disease **grew** / **spread** / **led** quickly among the children.
4 Mum didn't wake me up, so it was her **tradition** / **fault** / **effect** that I missed the bus.
5 Don't cry. You have to be **brave** / **helpful** / **secret** now.
6 The police caught the young man who had **wasted** / **confused** / **committed** the crime.
7 The guard took out his **cart** / **gun** / **treason** and stopped the man.
8 People were shocked when the bomb **went off** / **shook** / **bled** near the station.

2 WORDS What's the verb?

____ / 16

Look at the pictures and write down the infinitives of the verbs that go with them. (8P)

1 ________ 2 ________ 3 ________ 4 ________

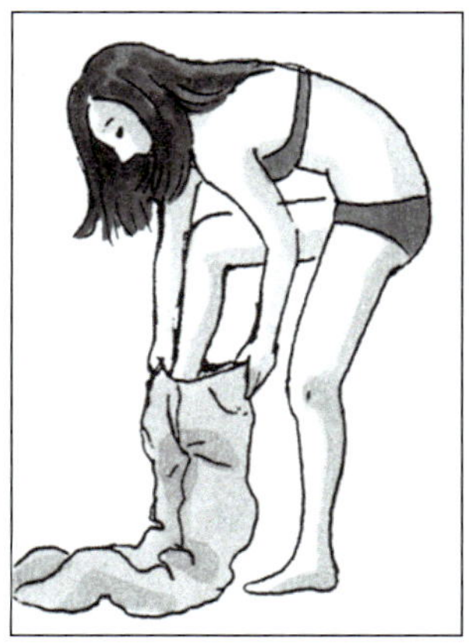

5 ________ 6 ________ 7 ________ 8 ________

Now you

Write at least eight sentences in your exercise book using the verbs above. (8P)

3 GRAMMAR At MIT

___ /7

You visit the Massachusetts Institute of Technology (MIT) in Boston and want to go on a guided tour there. At the beginning the guide tells you about the rules for the tour. After the tour you are chatting to a friend from England on the internet and tell her what the guide at MIT said.

> **Commands and request in indirect speech**
>
> Wenn du Aufforderungen oder Bitten in der indirekten Rede wiedergeben möchtest, dann kannst du dazu bestimmte Verben verwenden.
>
> tell sb. to do sth. / tell sb. not to do sth. (für Aufforderungen)
> ask sb. to do sth. / ask sb. not to do sth. (für Bitten)
>
> Beispiel: Annabel: 'Don't eat my cake!'
> Annabel **told** her sister **not to eat** her cake.

1 *Guide* 'Let the security guard[1] check your bags first.'

You The guide told us to ______________________

2 *Guide* 'Show your tickets at the gate.'

You She ______________________

3 *Guide* 'Don't leave the group during the tour.'

You ______________________

4 *Guide* 'Listen to me and don't talk.'

You ______________________

5 *Guide* 'Please don't eat or drink on the tour.'

You ______________________

6 *Guide* 'Please turn off your cellphones during the tour.'

You ______________________

7 *Guide* 'Please tell me if you have any questions.'

You ______________________

[1] security guard [sɪˈkjʊərəti ɡɑːd] *Wachpersonal*

4 GRAMMAR More about MIT

___/5

After the tour you can ask the guide questions. Tell your friend what you asked the guide.

Questions in indirect speech

- Bei Fragen **ohne Fragewort** wird die Frage in der indirekten Rede mit **if** oder **whether** eingeleitet.

  Beispiel: James asked: 'Do you like chocolate?'
  James asked me **if/whether** I liked chocolate.

- Bei Fragen **mit Fragewort** wird dieses auch in der indirekten Rede beibehalten.

  Beispiel: Rebecca asked: '**When** will I get my money back?'
  Rebecca wanted to know **when** she would get her money back.

1 'How many students have you got at MIT?'

I asked the guide ______________________________

2 'Do you know when the first scientist from MIT won a Nobel Prize?'

____

3 'Where do all the students live?'

____

4 'Why is MIT known all over the world?'

____

5 'Do you have any idea what the students will invent here in the future?'

____

5 GRAMMAR The Boston Public Garden

___/6

*The Boston Public Garden was opened in 1837 as the first botanical garden in the United States. Report what some people asked at the ticket office. Write the sentences in your exercise book. Use **asked** or **wanted to know** to start your sentences.*

1 An old man: 'Do you have wheelchairs?'
2 A mother: 'Can I feed my baby at the restaurant?'
3 An old woman: 'Did the garden really open in 1837?'
4 A boy: 'Will the garden be open during the winter?'
5 A family: 'Is there a play area for small children?'
6 A woman with a dog: 'Have you found a black purse?'

1 *An old man wanted to know if ...*

6 GRAMMAR A day in Boston

_____ / 8

Bobby has just spent four days in Boston. Look at his calendar to see what he did (✔) and didn't do (✘). Write ***conditional sentences (type 3)****.*

Thursday	Friday	Saturday	Sunday
Museum of Science / dinosaur film! ✘ Freedom trail (walking, 2.5 miles!) ✔	lunch at aunt Sally's house ✔ Quincy Market ✘	visit Egyptian exhibition / Museum of Fine Arts ✘ New England Aquarium / dolphins! ✔	Fenway Park Stadium ✔

Conditional sentences (type 3)	
If-clause: **past perfect**	Main clause: **conditional 2**
If he **had travelled** to Paris,	he **would have spoken** French a lot.
If they **had been** in Boston on Sunday,	they **could have seen** the Red Sox play.
If she **hadn't missed** the tour,	she **might have had** a good time.

1 If Bobby ____________________ (be) to the Museum of Science on Thursday,

he ____________________ (watch) a dinosaur film there.

2 If Bobby ____________________ (not have) on Friday,

he ____________________ (go).

3 If Bobby ____________________ (visit) on Saturday,

he ____________________ (not see) the sweet dolphins at the New England Aquarium.

4 If Bobby ____________________ (not be) to Fenway Park Stadium on Sunday,

he ____________________ (miss) a great baseball match.

MEDIATION

___/17

04 The book-printing machine

You are at Harvard Bookstore, a private bookstore near Harvard University in Boston, with a friend who doesn't speak English. He wants to find out more about Paige M. Gutenborg, the bookstore's new book-printing machine. Help him to speak to the assistant. Stop the recording when you hear the beep.

1 ***Your friend*** Kannst du bitte einen Verkäufer ansprechen, damit er uns diese neue Buchdruckmaschine zeigt?

You Excuse me, can you show us the new book-printing machine?

2 ***Assistant*** [Tonaufnahme abspielen bis zum ersten Hinweiston.]

You ______________________________

3 ***Your friend*** Welche Bücher kann die Maschine denn drucken?

You ______________________________

4 ***Assistant*** [Tonaufnahme abspielen bis zum zweiten Hinweiston.]

You ______________________________

____

____

5 ***Your friend*** Kann die Maschine nur englische oder auch anderssprachige Bücher drucken?

You ______________________________

____

6 ***Assistant*** [Tonaufnahme abspielen bis zum dritten Hinweiston.]

You ______________________________

____

7 *Your friend* Und ist die Qualität der Bücher irgendwie schlechter als normale Bücher?

You ______________________________

8 *Assistant* *[Tonaufnahme abspielen bis zum vierten Hinweiston.]*

You ______________________________

____

9 *Your friend* Und wie lange dauert es, bis ein Buch fertig ist? Könnte ich es gleich mitnehmen?

You ______________________________

____

10 *Assistant* *[Tonaufnahme abspielen bis zum fünften Hinweiston.]*

You ______________________________

____

____

11 *Your friend* Und was kostet ein Buch?

You ______________________________

12 *Assistant* *[Tonaufnahme abspielen bis zum sechsten Hinweiston.]*

You ______________________________

____

13 *Your friend* Nein, lass mal. Das ist nicht so wichtig. Ich wollte nur wissen, wie alles funktioniert. Sag vielen Dank.

You ______________________________

____

SPEAKING

___/26

05 Finding out about a museum

Listen to the phone call between a teenager and Tracy, a woman working at the Boston Children's Museum.

> Höre dir das Telefonat an und notiere die Formulierungen, die hilfreich sein könnten, wenn du im **Now you** selbst Fragen stellst.

06 Now you

Imagine you and your family are staying in Boston. You are thinking of going to the New England Aquarium.

a) *Look at the notes and write down the questions to prepare for your own phone call. (13P)*

b) *Now ring the museum and ask your questions. (13P)*

Stop the recording when you hear the beep. Continue listening when you have said your part.

every day / Monday?
opening times?
tickets?
little sister (2 years) – ticket?
guided tours?
price?
how long?
how to get there?
car?
special events?
thank you

Jason Hi! This is the New England Aquarium. My name is Jason. How can I help you?

You Hello, my name is ... I have a few questions.

Klassenarbeit B

Gesamtpunktzahl ______ / 80 Note ______

LISTENING

______ / 26

07 **Martha's Vineyard**

Listen to the podcast about Martha's Vineyard, an island off the coast of Massachusetts in the Atlantic Ocean.

1 Sights on Martha's Vineyard

______ / 6

Now look at the list and decide in which order the places appear in the recording.

a) Aquinnah Cliffs		d) Vineyard Haven	
b) Flying Horse Carousel		e) Wampanaog Tribal Center	
c) Moshup Beach		f) West Tisbury	

2 More information on Martha's Vineyard

______ / 20

Read the following sentences, then listen again. Is the information right, wrong or not in the text? Tick the correct boxes.

		Right	Wrong	Not in the text
1 The podcast was designed ...	a) to give information about Martha's Vineyard.			
	b) to keep children happy during the crossing.			
2 Martha's Vineyard is great for shopping because ...	a) things are sold really cheaply there.			
	b) there's a nice flea market in Edgartown.			
	c) you can buy really nice souvenirs at the general store in West Tisbury.			
3 Moshup Beach ...	a) is in the west of the island.			
	b) is the best beach on the island.			
	c) is where the horror film 'Jaws' was filmed.			
4 The Wampanoag ...	a) are the only people who always live on Martha's Vineyard.			
	b) moved to the island in the 19th century.			
	c) celebrated the first Thanksgiving[1] with the pilgrims.			
5 President Obama ...	a) owns a large house on Martha's Vineyard.			
	b) has been to Martha's Vineyard as a tourist.			
	c) is one of the famous people who might be seen there.			
6 The Flying Horses Carousel ...	a) is the oldest of its kind in the USA.			
	b) is over 200 years old.			
	c) is a great ride for young and old.			
7 This ferry takes tourists to ...	a) Chilmark.			
	b) Vineyard Haven.			
	c) East Chop Lighthouse.			

[1] Thanksgiving [ˌθæŋksˈgɪvɪŋ] *Danksagung*

WRITING

____/14

The travel blog

You've spent a weekend on Martha's Vineyard and have written down some notes about your stay. Look at the map and notes and write an entry for your blog.

Write about 100–140 words.

You can choose from the notes – don't write about everything!

How to get there
- *by ferry (Vineyard Haven or Edgartown)*
- *by plane (Martha's Vineyard Airport)*

Getting around
- *by bus*
- *by car*

Places to stay
- *MV family campground*
- *seaside hotel at Oak Bluffs*

Places to visit:

Tisbury
- *tourist information (→ guide book, information about bus times, the island, tourist attractions)*

Oak Bluffs
- *Flying Horse Carousel*
- *The Arts District (→ nice poster)*

Chilmark
- *The Meadow Flea Market (→ old wooden box)*

Wampanoag Tribal Center
- *found out lots about the Wampanoag – First Thanksgiving!*

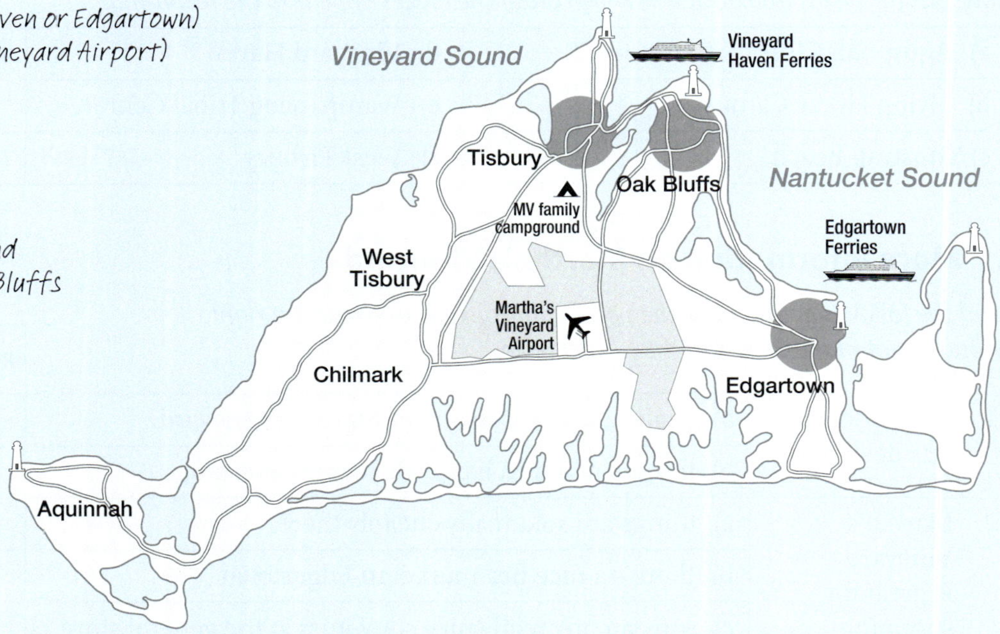

Say something about …

- how you arrived at Martha's Vineyard.
- how you got from place to place.
- where you went shopping and what you bought.
- what you took photos of.
- where you spent the night.
- what the weather was like.
- what you liked doing and why.

How to write your text

- Organize your ideas with the help of the list above before you start writing.
- Structure your text (beginning, middle, end).
- Use topic sentences.
- Use linking words and phrases.
- Use adjectives and adverbs.
- Correct your text (spelling, grammar).

You can begin your blog like this:

Hi folks. I'm back from Martha's Vineyard and …

LANGUAGE

___ / 40

1 WORDS Synonyms

___ / 8

Find synonyms for the underlined words. Be careful that you write down the correct forms.

1 The <u>win</u> over the Red Sox was very important for the Yankees. ______________________

2 The white people brought a lot of <u>illnesses</u> to America. ______________________

3 The tourists were happy when they finally reached a nice <u>tavern</u>. ______________________

4 Could you <u>pick me up</u> from the airport, please? ______________________

5 The first <u>colonists</u> had very hard lives. ______________________

6 Poor people in poor countries often live in <u>small houses</u>. ______________________

7 I have got <u>some</u> interesting books about Boston. ______________________

8 The guard <u>shouted</u> at the prisoner. ______________________

2 WORDS Farming

___ / 10

Fill in the correct words. Be careful: there are more words than you need.

agriculture • beans • cart • goats • (to) grow • harvest • (to) milk • smoke • soil • to spread • spring • treason • turkey

1 You have to have a garden if you want to ______________ your own vegetables.

2 If the ______________ in your garden isn't very good, it's difficult to grow ______________.

3 When it is ______________ time, the corn is ready to be eaten.

4 You can use a ______________ to transport all your tools to your garden and back home.

5 If we couldn't see all the ______________ coming from our neighbours' garden, we wouldn't know they were having a barbecue.

6 There was an interview with an American farmer on the news. He was talking about the problems in ______________ in his country.

7 It's great to have a ______________ in your garden if you need to water your plants.

8 The first thing the farmer does in the morning is ______________ his ______________.

3 GRAMMAR What would have been different?

____ / 10

Put the correct sentence halves together. Write ***conditional sentences (type 3)*** *in your exercise book.*

1 If the guided tour on Martha's Vineyard (finish) earlier, ...	a) nobody (scream).
2 If the museum staff members (keep an eye on) the teenagers, ...	b) the bow (not be stolen) from the exhibition in Edgartown.
3 If the Indian (not tie) the goat to the fence with a rope, ...	c) the family (not miss) the ferry back to Quonset Point.
4 If the gun (not go off) at the 4th of July parade, ...	d) the pretty cottages (be destroyed).
5 If the fire (spread) more quickly around Oak Bluffs, ...	e) it (keep) eating the corn in the garden.

1 *If the guided tour on Martha's Vineyard had finished earlier, ...*

4 GRAMMAR On the ferry

____ / 12

Lots of people were on the ferry to Martha's Vineyard. The Vanderhook family was there too. Cathy Vanderhook doesn't like ferry journeys and she spent a lot of time sitting in the corner, feeling sick. After the trip her family told her what people had said on the ferry.

Write the questions and orders in indirect speech. Write the sentences in your exercise book.

1 A young man on a bike asked: 'How far is it from Oak Bluffs to Edgartown and back?'
2 The young boy was wondering: 'Mom, have you been to Martha's Vineyard before?'
3 The young woman wanted to know: 'Will somebody from the hotel fetch us from the ferry?'
4 The 15-year-old girl told her mother: 'Don't give me a hug in front of everybody!'
5 A young couple asked two students: 'Are you going to enjoy a day at Moshup Beach too?'
6 The mother told her son: 'Stop screaming!'
7 The passenger asked another man: 'Can you keep an eye on my dog for a minute?'
8 A German tourist wanted to know: 'Is it worth going on the African-American Heritage Trail?'
9 An African-American told the tourists: 'You must visit the place where Captain William Martin is buried!'
10 An old woman asked: 'Who was Captain William Martin?'
11 The teenager wanted to know from his girlfriend: 'Did you have to wait long for me at the ferry?'
12 A journalist asked: 'When was The Flying Horses Carousel moved to Oak Bluffs?'

1 *The young man on a bike asked how far ...*

Edgartown Lighthouse

Gesamtpunktzahl ohne Speaking ______ / 73 Note ______
Gesamtpunktzahl mit Speaking ______ / 90 Note ______

LISTENING

______ / 17

08 **Which is the best school trip – Yosemite National Park or San Diego?**

Class 8B and their teacher Mrs Astbury from Goldwater High School in Phoenix, Arizona are talking about their school trip. One group wants to go to Yosemite National Park, another group wants to go on a trip to San Diego, California.

1 The San Diego presentation

______ / 4

Look at the photos. Listen to the text and put the four activities in the order they are talked about. Be careful: there are more photos than you need.

New words
ghost tour ['gəʊst tʊə(r)] *Geistertour*

A

B

C

D

E

F

2 Who in the class?

____ / 10

Listen again and tick (✔) the correct answers. Be careful: there are always two correct answers.

1 The first group ...	a) has already presented its ideas.	
	b) are mostly girls.	
	c) talked about Yosemite National Park.	
	d) wants to stay in a hostel.	
2 The teacher ...	a) has visited Yosemite National Park.	
	b) talks about last week's presentation.	
	c) wants to go to San Diego.	
	d) tells everyone to listen to the second presentation.	
3 The second group ...	a) wants to go sailing in San Diego.	
	b) wants to go on a special tour.	
	c) thinks that the beach is a good place to relax.	
	d) wants to go on a 30-minute boat trip.	
4 The second group ...	a) has already planned activities for the evenings.	
	b) offers to talk to a surf school about lessons.	
	c) has got more work to do if the class decides to go to San Diego.	
	d) already knows about a special group price at the zoo.	
5 The class ...	a) could go on a boat tour of San Diego harbour.	
	b) has no questions about the San Diego trip.	
	c) can't decide.	
	d) has to decide on Tuesday.	

3 Things to do

____ / 3

The second group will have to do some organizing if the class decides to go to San Diego.
Make notes about three of the jobs they talk about.

School Trip to San Diego

To do list

____

____

____

LANGUAGE

_____ / 33

1 WORDS Questions about the trip to San Diego

_____ / 8

The students are talking about the trip to San Diego. Complete their sentences with words from the box. Be careful: there are more words than you need.

advantages • bilingual • comment • desert • governor • migrant workers • minority • ocean • pollution • vineyard • wealthy

1 Is San Diego at the ______________________? Are there a lot of nice beaches?

2 Is air ______________________ very bad in San Diego?

3 Who is the ______________________ of California?

4 Is San Diego a poor city or a ______________________ one?

5 What are the ______________________ of this trip over the trip to Yosemite National Park?

6 Is it true that there are a lot of ______________________ in San Diego?

7 How many ______________________ people live in San Diego? What languages do they speak?

8 Do you think that the people in the class who want to go to San Diego are in the ______________?

2 WORDS Wrapeasy[1] – a new application

_____ / 5

*Add **-ful** or **-less** to the words in the box and complete the sentences. Be careful: there are more words than you need. Be careful about the spelling.*

beauty • end • event • forget • hope • sleep • use

- You don't know how to make a present for your friends and family look nice?

  Are you ______________ with wrapping paper[2]?
- Does it give you ______________ nights when you've been invited to a party?
- Our new application will help you to make your presents look ______________.
- It's not like all those other ______________ applications that don't really help anybody.
- Wrapeasy gives you ______________ ideas of what to do with books, CDs, games,

  special presents and even money. You'll always find something new.
- Simply wrapeasy!

[1] wrap- [ræp] *hier: einzuwickeln* [2] wrapping paper ['ræpɪŋ peɪpə(r)] *Geschenkpapier*

3 GRAMMAR Who's who in class 8B?

___ /4

A new teacher is asking Mrs Astbury who is who in the class.
Look at the picture and write Mrs Astbury's answers. Use the ***present participle****.*

Participle clauses instead of relative clauses

Das **present participle** kann einen Relativsatz im Aktiv ersetzen. Dadurch wird der Satz kürzer.

The girl	**who is sitting** next to me		is my friend Carla.
The girl	**sitting** next to me		is my friend Carla.

1 Who's Sue? *She's the girl sitting in front of the window.*

2 Who's Maria? ______________________________

3 Who's Tom? ______________________________

4 Who's Amira? ______________________________

5 Who's Hector? ______________________________

4 GRAMMAR The school trip

___ /5

Complete the sentences about the San Diego presentation. Use the ***present perfect passive****.*

The passive: present perfect

Bildung: has/have + been + past participle

Most animals	**have**	already	**been**	**fed**	this morning.
A new zebra	**has**		**been**	**bought**	for the zoo.

1 Different ideas ______________________________ (present) to the class.

2 A map ______________________________ (draw) on the board.

3 Two different activities ______________________________ (talk about) for the last day of the trip.

4 The zoo tour ______________________________ (not describe) very well.

5 The class ______________________________ (not ask) to decide on the trip right now.

5 GRAMMAR Preparations for the trip

____ / 6

What do Mrs Astbury and the students talk about before the trip?

The passive: will-future / modals

Bildung: will/modal + be + past participle

A lot of questions **will be asked** at the parents' evening.
The match **may be watched** by a lot of people.

1 ***Mrs A.*** All your bags ________________ (should / pack) the evening before we leave.

2 ***A student*** ________________ (can / the money / pay) after the trip?

3 ***Mrs A.*** If you make trouble during the trip, your parents ________________ (will / call).

4 ***Mrs A.*** You ________________ (might / ask) to show your ID at the hotel, so please bring it.

5 ***Mrs A.*** Our bus ________________ (could / hold up) in the traffic, so bring enough food and drink.

6 ***A student*** ________________ (will / we / pick up) in front of the school?

6 GRAMMAR After the trip

____ / 5

*A lot of interesting things happened during the trip. Jeremy has collected some facts for the year book. He has dropped some juice on his note paper so he can't read all the information now. Write his sentences in the **passive** so he doesn't need the missing information.*

1  told the group about a poltergeist in their hotel.

The group ________________.

2  showed the girls a trained monkey.

The girls ________________.

3  gave Martin a personal surf lesson on the beach.

Martin ________________.

4  offered the group free tickets for a comedy show.

The group ________________.

5  sent Mrs Astbury a funny text message.

Mrs Astbury ________________.

MEDIATION

____/23

Come on our ghost tour!

Before you start
Sieh dir vor dem Lesen die Aufgabenstellung auf S. 43 an.

Would you like to meet real ghosts and learn their stories? Then come on our ghost tour to hear the scary and tragic stories of people who lived in San Diego one or two centuries ago. Meet Jim who was hanged for stealing a rowboat in 1852. Hear Anna crying for her lost children. These are some of the sad stories of people who lived in California long ago.

You will be led around by a "Ghost Hunter" who doesn't seem to see the ghosts that our visitors always see. Learn San Diego's sad stories and meet some real ghosts who have come back to tell their stories – sometimes in a funny way, but sometimes in a spooky way.

Tours are limited to 50 people. Two tours are offered every Friday and Saturday night. The first tour begins at 6.30 pm and the second tour begins at 7.00 pm. We ask you to arrive at the Visitor Information Center about 15 minutes before the start of the tour.

Information

Tour Name:
Ghost Tours

Event Dates:
Friday and Saturday evenings

Event Times:
Performances at 6.30 pm and 7.00 pm.

Cost:
Adults: $10 per ticket, children under 13: $5.00. Special prices are offered on the first and second Friday of each month but only for the first tour beginning at 6.30 pm. These prices are for groups with at least 12 people only. Reservations for these offers can only be made on the internet at the Brown Paper Tickets agency.

Tour Length:
1 hour

Tickets:
Visitor Information Center at Old Town San Diego State Historic Park.
Tickets are only sold on the day of the tour on a first-come-first-served basis.

Reservations:
www.brownpapertickets/events

Information:
619-220-5422

Webpage:
www.parks.ca.gov/oldtownsandiego

Du bist mit deiner Familie im Urlaub in San Diego, Kalifornien. Deine Großmutter hat im Hotel den Flyer über die Geistertouren gefunden. Da sie einiges darin nicht versteht, bittet sie dich um Hilfe.

a) *Lies den Flyer auf S. 42 und markiere im Text die Informationen zu folgenden Punkten:*
- *Was die „Ghost Tour" ist. (1P)*
- *Was das Besondere an der Führung ist. (1P)*
- *Details, die für deine Großmutter wichtig sein könnten (mind. sechs). Siehe dir z. B. die folgenden drei Bilder an. (5P)*

Markieren des Textes
Du kannst zum Markieren auch verschiedene Farben verwenden.
Das kann dir den Überblick erleichtern.

b) *Nun schreibe für deine Großmutter die wichtigsten Punkte aus dem Flyer auf.*
*Benutze dafür die Informationen, die du unter **a)** markiert hast. Schreibe vollständige Sätze. (11P)*

c) *Deine Großmutter hat auf dem Flyer etwas von **special prices** gelesen und dich gefragt, was damit gemeint ist. Sie denkt, dass eure Familie so vielleicht Geld sparen kann.*

*Erkläre deiner Oma, worum es sich bei diesen **special prices** handelt und ob das Angebot auf eure Familie zutrifft. (5P)*

SPEAKING

____ / 17

09 Getting information on the phone

The students have agreed on the school trip to San Diego. Today they are working on the programme for the trip. One student rings up a surf school in San Diego to find out more about surf lessons. Listen to the phone call.

☞ Lies dir zunächst die deutschen Informationen in **Now you** durch. Wenn du dir zutraust, diese Informationen ohne Hilfe zu verwenden, dann beginne sofort mit diesem Aufgabenteil. Ansonsten höre dir zunächst die Fragen und Antworten der Schülerin genau an. Sie helfen dir, wenn du in **Now you** die Rolle eines Schülers oder einer Schülerin übernimmst.

10 Now you

Imagine you are planning a visit to San Diego Zoo for your school trip. Phone the zoo and ask for information. Stop the recording when you hear the beep. Continue listening when you have said your part.

1 ***San Diego Zoo***

▼

You Sage, wer du bist und dass du von der Kennedy High School anrufst. Sage, dass du mit deiner Klasse nach San Diego kommst und den Zoo besuchen möchtest. (3P)

2 ***San Diego Zoo***

▼

You Bejahe die Frage und sage, dass eure Klassenfahrt vom 2.–5. Mai sein wird. (2P)

3 ***San Diego Zoo***

▼

You Frage nach den Öffnungszeiten des Zoos. (1P)

4 ***San Diego Zoo***

▼

You Frage, ob der Zoo eine Führung speziell für Schulklassen hat. (1P)

5 ***San Diego Zoo***

▼

You Sage, dass du in der 8. Klasse bist und dass ihr 30 Leute sein werdet: 28 Jugendliche und zwei Erwachsene. (3P)

6 ***San Diego Zoo***

▼

You Sage, dass das interessant klingt und frage, wie viel Zeit man für diese Führung benötigt. (2P)

7 ***San Diego Zoo***

▼

You Frage, um wie viel Uhr die Führung beginnt. (1P)

8 ***San Diego Zoo***

▼

You Du bist einverstanden. Frage, wie viel die Tour für die ganze Gruppe kostet. (2P)

9 ***San Diego Zoo***

▼

You Sage, dass du erst mit deinem Lehrer und der Klasse sprechen musst. Sage, dass du dich morgen wieder meldest. Verabschiede dich. (2P)

10 ***San Diego Zoo***

Gesamtpunktzahl ______ / 66 Note ______

READING

____ / 13

"Earthquakes[1]: we want to be prepared"

San Jose High School, San Diego, gets prepared for earthquakes

by our reporter Jack Simon

1
This year San Jose High School will take part in the earthquake safety exercise that is held every year all over California on the third Thursday of October. "Our school safety team is going to plan the activities," says head teacher Mr Nicola. "Here in California we're living in earthquake country – that's why parents, teachers and students have agreed to take part in earthquake safety day or "ESD", as it is called. We want to be prepared when the next earthquake comes."

2
The school's safety team has twelve members: parents, students and teachers. The safety team has met several times to work out a program for the big day in October. "Today we still don't know what the exercises on ESD will look like exactly," says Mrs Cast, teacher and member of the team. "But an important part of the exercise will be finding out how you can protect yourself if there is an earthquake, and practicing your reactions. A second part will be to get all of our 850 students to walk quietly out of the school building without panicking."

3
A first step was to ask parents to prepare an "earthquake bag" for their children to take to school. The "earthquake bag" should contain two bottles of water, two snacks, a card with the family contact information on it and a family photo. Parents may add one or two other things that they think might help their children in an earthquake. And the child's name must be clearly written on the bag. "At the end of the school year the bags will be given back – hopefully they'll be unused[2]," says Mr Nicola.

4
In the weeks before the exercise in October the teachers at San Jose High School will talk about earthquakes with their students. "There'll be different topics for the different ages: stories, games and quizzes for the younger students, surfing the internet and writing reports for the older ones," explains Mr Nicola. By the end of their time at San Jose, every student will know a lot about earthquakes worldwide and especially in California. "We hope that with our activities we can help more people to survive an earthquake," says Mr Nicola.

5
This report shows you – our readers – another good example of how people in California are trying to live with the dangers of earthquakes. We hope that this article makes you, your school or your office think what you could do. Why don't you join in and become part of the Californian program or start a program of your own?

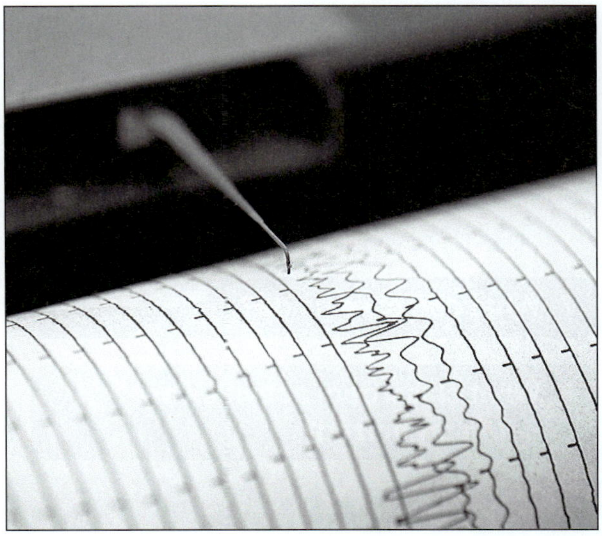

[1] earthquake ['ɜːθkweɪk] *Erdbeben* [2] unused [ʌn'juːzd] *unbenutzt*

1 Headings

_____ /5

Find headings for all five paragraphs of the newspaper article.

☞ Überschriften sind in der Regel kurz formuliert und keine ganzen Sätze.
Die Überschrift gibt dem Leser eine kurze Vorschau auf die Kernaussage eines Abschnittes.

1 ______________________

2 ______________________

3 ______________________

4 ______________________

5 ______________________

2 FAQ

_____ /8

San Jose High School's website has some FAQ (frequently asked questions[1]) about the school's earthquake safety day (ESD). Answer the questions with information from the newspaper article. You do not need to write complete sentences.

1 When is ESD? ______________________

2 How often is ESD? ______________________

3 Why have ESD at San Jose High School? ______________________

4 Who can be on the safety team? ______________________

5 What is the safety team's job? ______________________

6 What happens on ESD? (two things) ______________________

____

7 What can parents do? ______________________

8 What classroom activities are being organized? ______________________

[1] frequently asked questions [ˌfriːkwəntli ɑːskt ˈkwestʃənz] *häufig gestellte Fragen*

LANGUAGE

___/38

1 WORDS Earthquake safety (I)

___/8

Some letters are missing from this flyer on earthquake safety. Can you replace them?

Earthquake Safety Checklist

Before an earthquake

- *Don't take earthquake w_ _ _ _ _ _ _ as a joke.*
- *Remember your cellphones are u_ _ _ _ _ _ without electricity.*
- *Learn first aid[1] to help your family in an emergency. E_ _ _ _ _ for a first aid course now!*
- *Keep enough food and water in p_ _ _ _ _ _ bottles for three days.*

During an earthquake

- *S_ _ under furniture and don't move!*
- *P_ _ _ _ _ _ your head from falling objects.*

After an earthquake

- *Only call a police p_ _ _ _ _ if you really have to. They are very busy now.*
- *H_ _ _ _ _ _ _ _ _ should not go back into their houses before they know it's safe to do so.*

2 WORDS Earthquake safety (II)

___/10

In English you can replace the phrase ***he or she*** *by using* ***they****;* ***him or her*** *by using* ***them*** *or* ***his or her*** *by using* ***their****. Complete the following sentences.*

In flyers on earthquake safety you will read that everybody should leave ____________ house as quickly as possible. People can be buried alive if ____________ stay inside. If a person is too ill or too old to leave ____________ home, a relative should try to help ____________, but only if ____________ don't put themselves in danger. If somebody needs help, ____________ can call 911 for the emergency services and someone will soon be there to support ____________. Every emergency assistant is trained to do ____________ best in difficult situations and if ____________ tell you to do something, you should listen to ____________.

[1] first aid [ˌfɜːst ˈeɪd] *Erste Hilfe*

3 GRAMMAR San Jose High School and ESD

____ / 16

*A student from San Jose High School has written about ESD. Fill in the correct form of the verbs in brackets. Be careful: some of the sentences are **active**, some are **passive**.*

Once a year at every Californian school the things to *be done* (do) during an earthquake ________________ (practice). This day ________________ (call) ESD – Earthquake Safety Day. Last week it was ESD at San Jose High School. The day before ESD, we ________________ (ask) to bring our earthquake bags to school. I took my bag to school, and everyone in the class ________________ (tell) to keep their earthquake bags with them at all times because you never know when there could be an earthquake.

At 9.30 am the school bell rang and the ESD exercises ________________ (begin). Everyone ________________ (have to do) the exercises: teachers and students. When the bell rang, everybody ________________ (tell) to get on the floor under a table or desk. We waited on the floor for a few minutes until a sign ________________ (give). Then we all ________________ (stand up). The bell ________________ (ring) again and everyone ________________ (leave) the building quietly. Outside the building all the students ________________ (count). When the head teacher was sure that no one was left in the building, we ________________ (tell) to go back to our classes. And next year, all these things ________________ (will practice) again because there ________________ (will be) a lot of new, young students who don't know yet what ________________ (should do) during an earthquake.

4 GRAMMAR Earthquake!

_____/4

After an earthquake the emergency services are trying to get the situation under control. Write what they want the people to do. Write complete sentences.

Der Infinitiv mit to

Nach bestimmten Verben kann ein Object mit **to-infinitive** stehen: ask/help/invite/teach/ ... sb. (not) to do sth.

The emergency services **want people to listen** to them.

1 The police / would like / everybody / stay calm

____

2 The fire service / wants / drivers / keep the streets free

____

3 The paramedics / are asking / injured[1] people / go to hospital themselves if they can

____

4 The police / want / shop owners / stay close to their shops

____

WRITING

_____/15

Young firefighters California

Welcome to the young firefighters of California blog. This week it was ESD California again and we would like to hear from you about it.

Quencho, 15 (San Francisco)

I've been a member of the young firefighters for eight months and I was very excited about ESD this year. At school I helped with a class of younger students and explained to them what they should do if an earthquake happens. Then we practiced in the classroom. I think they had fun AND learned some very important things. After school I went to the local shopping center where we gave out flyers. Next year I want to join the adult firefighters and train so that I can rescue people from buildings which have collapsed.

Jackero, 17 (San Diego)

I've been reading all these blog entries and I want to say that ESD is absolute nonsense! I have had to survive so many ESDs and I still don't really know if I could do the right thing in an earthquake. Every year we do the same things, but if there really is an earthquake everything will be different anyway. And people will just panic no matter how many ESDs they have been through.

Add your own comment to the blog. Give your opinion on Quencho's or Jackero's comment and use what you know about fire practices[2] at your own school to explain what you think. Write about 100 words in your exercise book.

[1] injured ['ɪndʒəd] *verletzt* [2] fire practice ['faɪə(r) præktɪs] *(Probe-)Feueralarm*

Klassenarbeit A

Gesamtpunktzahl ______ / 101 Note ______

LISTENING

______ / 6

Announcements

11 ______ / 6

Listen to these lunchtime announcements at Hermann High, a high school in Hermann, Missouri. Then match the sentence halves. Be careful: there are more sentence halves than you need.

1 At Hermann High students aren't	a) sent home because they didn't obey the dress code[1].
2 Last week some students were	b) you must write your name on the bulletin board.
3 The FCCLA can help students to	c) asked to buy a copy of the dress code from the office.
4 The FCCLA's first project is to	d) allowed to wear hats or caps inside the school.
5 The King or Queen of the ball	e) to break the school rules.
6 If you want to be the King or Queen of the ball,	f) opens the school building for the dance.
	g) opens the dance.
	h) improve their leadership skills.
	i) stop fighting and bullying at Hermann High.

1		2		3		4		5		6	

LANGUAGE

______ / 47

1 WORDS Word building

______ / 6

*Often you can make a noun from a verb or an adjective by adding a **suffix**.*
*Find the correct **suffix** for each verb or adjective in the box on the left. Then write the nouns.*
Be careful with the spelling. (6P)

correct explain express ill real sad	-ation -ion -ity -ness

1 ______________________
2 ______________________
3 ______________________
4 ______________________
5 ______________________
6 ______________________

[1] dress code ['dres kəʊd] *Kleiderordnung*

2 WORDS A crossword

___/15

Complete the sentences and fill in the crossword.

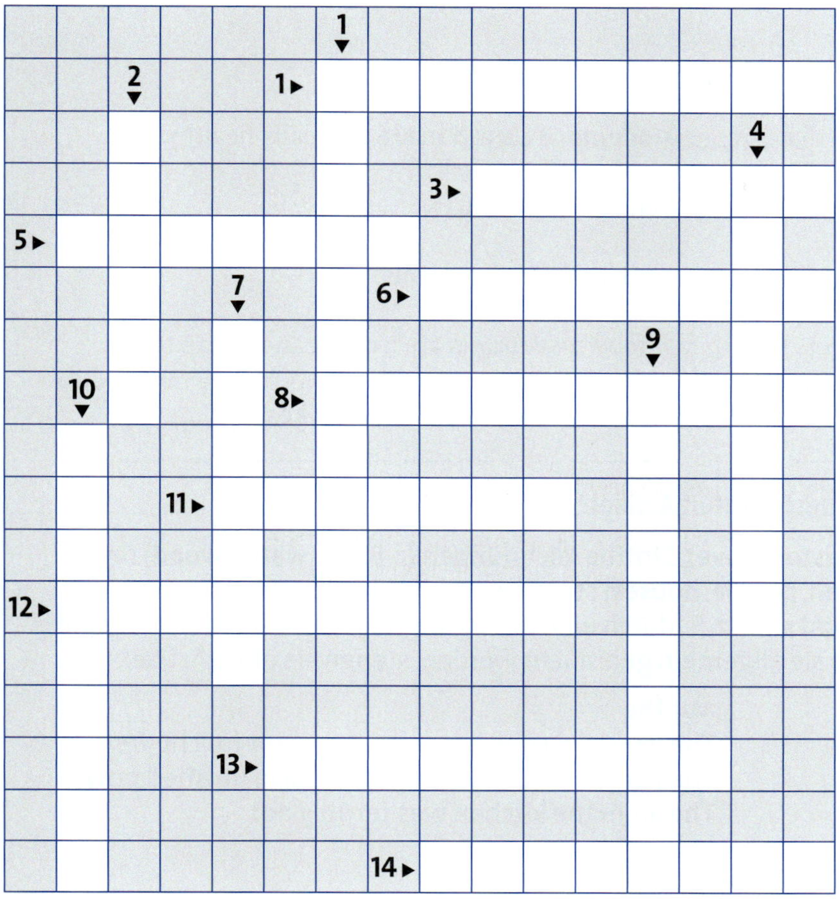

Across:

1 The 1906 ... destroyed San Francisco.
3 If you have toothache, go to the ... .
5 You can find the bulletin board in the ... .
6 Who's your ... in the next match?
8 The school offers many extracurricular ... .
11 Sausages taste much better with ... .
12 That's really ... . It can't be true!
13 He sticks all his postcards in a ... .
14 Lübeck is a UNESCO world ... city.

Down:

1 You often go red if you're ... .
2 Do you think people go to ... when they die?
4 At the end of a letter you can write: 'Yours ...'
7 I only read a ... of the report.
9 School is closed ... August.
10 Sorry, but the top isn't ... in your size.

San Francisco in 1906

3 GRAMMAR The health lesson

____ / 4

*In their Science lesson at Hermann High the students talked about healthy food. Here are some statements which the students and their teacher made. Read the sentences and add **the** where it is needed.*

1 We know that ______ young people often eat ______ fast food.

2 We are proud that ______ burgers that ______ students of class 8 made are really healthy.

3 Lots of ______ people work so much that they aren't able to cook.

4 Then they often eat ______ fast food and don't prepare their own meals.

5 Many people say that ______ burgers sold in fast-food restaurants are a quick and cheap lunch.

6 I don't like burgers. My favourite dish is ______ pizza that my sister often makes.

Mit bestimmtem oder ohne bestimmten Artikel?

Abstrakte Nomen (z. B. **life, history, love**), Stoffbezeichnungen (z. B. **air, water, wood**) und Nomen im Plural (z. B. **children, people, houses**) stehen nur dann mit bestimmtem Artikel (**the**), wenn sie näher bestimmt sind, z. B. durch eine **of**-Fügung, einen Relativsatz oder eine Orts- oder Zeitangabe. Wenn sie allgemein gebraucht werden, stehen sie ohne Artikel.

Ohne **the**	Mit **the**
Love is important for children.	**The** love of mothers is very important for children.
People need a lot of sleep.	**The** people who built the house have finished now.
We all need air to breathe.	**The** air in the kitchen was terribly hot.

4 GRAMMAR Countable or uncountable?

____ / 10

Look at the words in the box and decide if they are countable or uncountable nouns. Write them into the correct list.

ancestor • butter • clothing • copy • election • homework • meeting • mustard • original • winemaking

Countable nouns	Uncountable nouns

5 GRAMMAR After Susie's party

____ / 12

*Look at the picture. You can see Susie's table after a party. Complete the sentences under the picture. Use **many**, **much**, **a few** or **a little**.*

1 Susie's guests liked the sausages. There are only ________________ left.

2 They didn't eat ________________ bread. But David and Sandy ate ________________.

3 People didn't drink ________________ lemonade, but they had quite ________________ bottles of cola.

4 The guests didn't eat ________________ grapes.

5 Susie has still got ________________ apples on her table, but she hasn't got ________________ bananas left.

6 Susie has got ________________ cake left for the next day.

7 The guests liked Susie's potato salad. There isn't ________________ left.

8 But they didn't eat ________________ crisps. Maybe Susie got the wrong sort.

9 Susie is happy – there isn't too ________________ food left over from the party.

Zählbare und nicht zählbare Nomen

- **Countable nouns** sind zählbare Nomen, d.h. sie bezeichnen etwas, das man zählen kann. Es gibt sie im Singular und Plural. Sie können mit unbestimmtem Artikel (**a** book), Zahlwörtern (**three** books) und bestimmten Mengenangaben (**some** books, **a lot of** books, **many** books, **a few** books) stehen. Die meisten Nomen im Englischen sind zählbar.
- **Uncountable nouns** sind nicht zählbare Nomen. Hierzu gehören Stoffbezeichnungen, (**bread**, **water**) und viele abstrakte Begriffe (**love**, **information**). Sie stehen nie mit unbestimmtem Artikel oder Zahlwörtern, jedoch mit bestimmten Mengenangaben (**some** information, **a lot of** homework, how **much** furniture, **a little** water).

MEDIATION

____/12

The Culture[1] Club

Die Schülermitverantwortung (SMV) deiner Schule möchte Aktionen für die bessere Integration von Schülerinnen und Schülern aus anderen Kulturkreisen durchführen. Du interessierst dich für dieses Thema. Da du weißt, dass die USA sehr multikulturell sind, schaust du dich im Internet um und stößt auf die Webseite der Kansas City High School.

Hi everyone at KCHS!

We have founded a new club called The Culture Club in which we want to have fun getting to know each other's cultural backgrounds. The Culture Club wants to focus on the great ethnic diversity at KCHS! The United States is a nation of immigrants, and at KCHS we would like to make everyone more aware of our different backgrounds. What languages do you speak at home? Have you, your parents, grandparents or great-grandparents immigrated to the United States from a far-away country? Have you got an unusual, exciting or perhaps a sad story to tell?

This year we a want to focus on two main activities. First of all we would like to make a big collection of posters to hang on the wall in the main hallway where as many different cultures, languages and countries of origin[2] as possible are presented. So, for example, if your family has come from China and you know some other students with the same background – get together, join the Culture Club and design a poster which will make your families proud.

The second activity this year is very special. We want to organize the food for this year's spring ball and have a buffet with ethnic food so that we can all taste and enjoy the delicious well-known or secret specialties from different countries. We need quite a lot of people to help us with this. We want to collect all the recipes in a little booklet which people can buy during the ball. Then maybe they can even try and cook some new meals at home.

And if all goes well this year – we already have some ideas for next year's activities. How about designing a new part of our school website where we show that we are proud of all the different ethnic groups here at KCHS? Tell us what you think about it! Or would you like to learn a new language – why not find a language tandem partner? You can teach each other your native languages. It won't cost you a cent and it could be a really amazing experience.

So hey, you out there! Are you proud of your family history? Have you got an interesting story to tell? Would you like to share your grandmother's favorite recipe with us? Come and meet us. We meet in room 7H every Thursday lunchtime.

Notiere dir Stichpunkte in dein Lernheft für die nächste SMV-Sitzung, so dass du deine Mitschülerinnen und Mitschüler über folgende Punkte informieren kannst:

- *Was ist der Culture Club der KCHS? Was ist sein Programm? (3P)*
- *An wen richtet er sich? (3P)*
- *Was bietet der Culture Club für das laufende Schuljahr an? Nenne die Aktivitäten (2P) und gib Beispiele, was im Einzelnen geplant ist (2P).*
- *Welche Ideen hat der Culture Club für die Zukunft? (2P)*

[1] culture ['kʌltʃə(r)] *Kultur* [2] origin ['ɒrɪdʒɪn] *hier: Herkunfts-*

STUDY SKILLS

___/36

WRITING A SUMMARY At the Maifest in Hermann

It all began at the Maifest in Hermann, Missouri last year. I was visiting my cousin Derek for the weekend. I had met him a few times at family parties, but I had never been to Hermann before. Before I went I spoke to Derek on the phone. "Hey Jane," he said, "It's great that you can come and stay. It's the perfect time of year to visit Hermann, because the Maifest is on!" I wasn't sure what he meant so I asked him. "OK, but what is the Maifest? I have never heard of it before." Derek laughed. "I can tell that you have never been to Hermann before. Everyone who knows Hermann knows the Maifest. It's a festival with traditional German dancing, bratwurst and beer." "German dancing? I'm not sure ...," I said. "Don't worry," Derek said, "It's good fun for everyone!"

When I arrived in Hermann by bus, Derek was there to meet me. The journey had been very long, and I was a little bit tired. Derek was very excited and, while we were walking towards his parents' house, he talked nonstop. "OK, the plan for tonight is to go to City Park for some fun rides with some friends of mine from high school. But before we go there we are meeting at Peter's house, he's probably my best friend, and after that ..." I smiled as I tried to keep up with him and said, "Derek – I only just arrived. Give me a break!"

Derek let me have a little break at home where his mom, my aunt Gracie, gave us some cookies and something to drink. At the kitchen table she explained about the old tradition of the Maifest. "Hermann has been celebrating the Maifest since the early 1870s when the event was an end-of-school picnic. Children dressed up in their best Sunday clothes and marched behind the band, which played traditional German music. Later in City Park the children were given knackwurst and pink lemonade!" "Oh please Mom, no history lesson now – we need to go." "OK, have fun tonight," said Gracie as we left the house.

The evening went on as Derek had said before. After we had met everybody at Peter's house, we went to City Park and had a good time there. The evening was great but what I will always remember is the moment when Peter's grandpa came along and said "Guten Abend!" to us. At first I didn't understand but then I realized that he was speaking German. Later Peter explained that his ancestors had come to Hermann from Germany and that until World War I, German was the main language spoken in Hermann. "We still speak German at home!" Peter explained. Then he smiled at me and I was a little bit embarrassed because this cute guy was looking right at me and I was sure I was going all red in the face. When we were walking to City Park, Peter was next to me and we started talking about our favorite music and our hobbies. Peter looked at me surprised when I told him that I loved cycling. "One day I would like to take my bike to Europe and cross the Alps[1] by bike," I said. He smiled at me and I smiled back. "You won't believe me when I tell you that I have a map of the Alps on the wall in my room!" he told me.

Peter and I have been chatting every day since that Maifest weekend, about bikes, tours and everything else and – well, maybe one day I will learn some German too.

Read the story and summarize it.

a) *What are the most important events of the story?* ***Who*** *did* ***what when, where*** *and* ***why****? Make some notes. (18P)*

b) *Use your notes and write a summary of about 10 sentences. (18P)*

☞ **Wichtige Punkte für die Inhaltsangabe**

- Sie ist kürzer als der Originaltext.
- Einleitung: Wovon handelt der Text (ein bis zwei Sätze)?
- Die wichtigsten Ereignisse nennen: Wer hat was wann, wo und warum gemacht?
- Schreibe im **simple present** und in eigenen Worten!
- Verwende keine direkte Rede, nenne keine Beispiele.

You can start you summary like this:

The story is set in May last year. Jane goes to Hermann, ...

[1] the Alps [ælps] *die Alpen*

Klassenarbeit B

Gesamtpunktzahl ohne Speaking ______	/ 84	Note ______
Gesamtpunktzahl mit Speaking ______	/ 111	Note ______

READING

____ / 20

An article from the St. Louis High School students' magazine

Drunk Driver Kills High School Friend In Car Accident

Wouldn't this headline make you SADD?

Of course it would. A headline like this would make anyone sad – luckily it's not real. But more than 2000 teenagers lose their lives on the road every year because of drunk driving. Drivers lose control over their cars and someone gets badly hurt or even killed.

Did you find that mistake in the subheading of this article? Actually there isn't one! But why is "sad" spelled "SADD"? The students at St. Louis High School now all know what stands behind this abbreviation – Students Against Destructive[1] Decisions[2]. A new group has formed at StLHS which wants to help all students to make the right decisions in life – especially about drinking alcohol, the use of drugs[3], dangerous driving and other teen problems. Gerald Masicz founded this group after he had heard about SADD from his cousin in Nebraska. "When I heard about SADD, I thought right away that it would be great if we had a SADD group at St. Louis High too. We all know how easy it can be to make the wrong decision at some point and we don't think enough about the effects some decisions can have on our future and other people." Gerald Masicz founded the SADD group with the help of the SADD organization. When asked why it was a good idea for teenagers to tell other teenagers about the dangers of alcohol, legal and illegal drugs, he said, "It's much easier for people of the same age to pass on this information because students don't want to be told by adults what to do. We don't tell anybody what to do or what not to do. We pass on information so people can make the right decisions themselves." The staff at StLHS are very happy about this new student group, and head teacher Aron Lesly said, "We are thankful for Gerald's help and his group's work and would like to give them all the support they need." The group's first project has been to get as many students and their parents as possible to sign the Contract[4] for Life. In this contract the students promise not to drink alcohol or take drugs and they also promise to be careful drivers and not to get into a car with someone who is unable to drive. The parents, for example, promise to always organize a safe lift home for their sons or daughters. "We have given one of the contracts to each of our 800 students and so far 350 have signed it. We hope there will be many more," Gerald said.

The members of the new club at StLHS hope to be positive role models for other students. So let's hope that all students make careful decisions and that today's headline won't have to become reality.

http://www.sadd.org/

[1] destructive [dɪ'strʌktɪv] *destruktiv, zerstörerisch* [2] decision [dɪ'sɪʒn] *Entscheidung*
[3] drug [drʌg] *Droge* [4] contract ['kɒntrækt] *Vertrag*

1 Headings

____/ 10

a) There are no paragraphs in the main part of the text (lines 5–32).
Use a pen and divide the main part of the text into five paragraphs. Write the line numbers. (5P)

1	5–	2		3		4		5	

b) Then choose a heading for each paragraph from the following six.
Be careful: there is one more heading than you need. (5P)

Students help students | **Information for parents** | **What the teachers think**

The group's founder[1] | **Contract for Life** | **A new group at StLHS**

1 ______________________________

2 ______________________________

3 ______________________________

4 ______________________________

5 ______________________________

2 About the article

____/ 10

Find out if the information in the sentences is right, wrong or not in the text.

		Right	Wrong	Not in the text
1	Everyone at StLHS knows the SADD group now.			
2	Gerald's cousin is a member of a SADD group in Nebraska.			
3	A teenager was killed in a car accident in Nebraska the week before.			
4	Gerald has been on a SADD training course.			
5	The idea of SADD is that students give information to other students.			
6	SADD makes lots of rules for teenagers.			
7	The teachers think that the SADD group is a good idea.			
8	The Contract for Life has to be signed by two teenagers.			
9	SADD is an organization for parents.			
10	The majority of students haven't signed the contract.			

[1] founder ['faʊndə(r)] *Gründer/in*

LANGUAGE

____/35

1 WORDS Word building

____/8

a) *Often you can make a new word by putting two words together. Find the matching pairs in the two boxes and write them down. Be careful about the spelling (e.g. migrant worker, sub-heading).*

bulletin • earth • elementary • hall • home • scrap • see • sister	board • book • city • land • quake • school • through • way

1 ____________________ 5 ____________________

2 ____________________ 6 ____________________

3 ____________________ 7 ____________________

4 ____________________ 8 ____________________

b) *Write eight sentences with the new words from* ***a)****. Write them in your exercise book.*

2 GRAMMAR A big day for SADD

____/9

Simple present mit futurischer Bedeutung

Für Ereignisse, die in der Zukunft liegen, kannst du das **simple present** benutzen, wenn das Ereignis Teil eines Kalenders oder Zeitplans ist.

Beispiel: The train **leaves** tomorrow at 3 o'clock.

The SADD group at StLHS has planned a big event to get even more students to sign the Contract for Life. On the day before Gerald and Craigh are going through the programme. Use the ***simple present*** *to complete the following dialogue.*

Gerald Let's check the program. When do ____________________ (we / start)?

Craigh We ____________________ (begin) at 9 o'clock, half an hour later than usual.

Gerald OK, fine. When ____________________ (the head teacher / speak)?

Craigh Well, he ____________________ (be) on at ten past nine.

Then Lucy Smith ____________________ (open) the day a few minutes later.

She is the mother of the student who was hurt in that accident.

Gerald Right. When ____________________ (the workshops / begin)?

Craigh The student workshops ____________________ (start) at 9.30.

There ____________________ (be) some workshops in the afternoon too for parents.

The last workshop ____________________ (end) at 5 o'clock.

Gerald Great. I'm really looking forward to tomorrow.

3 GRAMMAR At my German school

____/7

*Sarah from St. Louis spent a year at a school in Stuttgart. She has written about her exchange year for the students' magazine at StLHS. Add **the** where it is needed.*

When I lived in Stuttgart, ______ school played an important part in my daily life. I really liked ______ school I went to. Usually in ______ Germany ______ lessons start very early in the morning, but ______ lessons at my school didn't start before 7.50. Lucky me! ______ History was my favorite class. I'm interested in ______ history, especially in ______ history of Germany after the Second World War.

I didn't really miss much about ______ US while I was there. But one thing I did miss was ______ extracurricular sports activities at school. The Germans like ______ sport, but they don't have school teams. If you want to play ______ sports, you have to join a club. If you like ______ soccer[1], you can watch matches every Saturday afternoon. I often went to watch VFB Stuttgart, ______ local team, play.

4 GRAMMAR Thoughts and questions about SADD

____/12

*Some students are interested in SADD. Look at the students' thoughts and questions and underline the correct quantifier **much**, **many**, **a few** or **a little**.*

1 How **many** / **much** wrong decisions[1] have I made in my life?

2 **A few** / **A little** of my friends have already made dangerous decisions in their lives.

3 How **many** / **much** money does it cost to become a member of SADD?

4 I have got **a few** / **a little** friends who are already members of SADD.

5 I want to have as **many** / **much** information as possible about SADD.

6 SADD is great – everybody should spend **a few** / **a little** time thinking about their decisions.

7 There have been **many** / **much** new stories about teenage problems on TV lately.

8 Even **a few** / **a little** alcohol is too **many** / **much** if you are driving.

9 I think **many** / **much** accidents would not have happened if more young people had known about SADD.

10 I have **a few** / **a little** questions about SADD. Who can I talk to?

11 How **many** / **much** times a week are there SADD meetings?

[1] soccer ['sɒkə(r)] *Fußball*

WRITING

____/15

An essay competition

You are spending a year at StLHS. At the Culture Club meeting you have been given the following flyer and have decided to take part in the competition. Write your essay in your exercise book.

☞ Bevor du beginnst, lies den gesamten Flyer noch einmal durch und entscheide, welche Informationen du verwenden möchtest. Mache dir auch Gedanken, wie du selbst zu den jeweiligen Punkten stehst und was du persönlich dazu schreiben kannst.

Mache dir einen Plan, wie du deinen Aufsatz aufbauen willst. Dabei können dir die **Steps of Writing** aus deinem Schülerbuch helfen (S. 168).

Wenn du sprachliche Hilfestellung benötigst, sieh dir noch einmal das **Skills File** auf S. 168/169 zum **Writing Course** an.

HELLO! HALLO! HOLA! SALUT! HEJ!

Can you say more than just hello in any language other than your own?

We think that foreign languages can open the door to the world!
Don't you agree?
But foreign languages are in danger in the United States of America!
Many American schools are giving up teaching foreign languages. Can you believe it?

We, The Institute of Foreign Language Teaching, are trying to fight back.
We are holding an essay writing competition.

Topic: Why foreign languages should be taught at all schools.

Tell us what you think. Share your experiences with foreign languages with us.

There are great prizes to win.
First prize: A four-week course in a foreign language of your choice.
Flights, four weeks in a hotel and all teaching materials are included.

Your essay should be about 200 words long.

Send it to The Institute of Foreign Language Teaching, Cleveland, OH, USA.

SPEAKING

____/27

12 Calling your exchange partner

Listen to the telephone call between Moritz from Germany and his American exchange partner Mike.

☞ Höre dir Moritz' Antworten an, halte die Tonaufnahme an und sprich sie abschnittsweise nach. Falls du etwas nicht verstehst, höre den Abschnitt noch einmal an. Wenn du mehr Hilfe benötigst, findest du den Hörtext in den Lösungen.

Notiere hilfreiche Formulierungen aus den Antworten in Stichpunkten in dein Lernheft. Deine Notizen helfen dir bei deinen eigenen Antworten in **Now you**.

13 Now you

Jason Winter, an American high school student from Hermann, Missouri, has written to your school. Your family has invited him to stay with you from August until January next school year. He's calling you to talk about the exchange. Stop the recording when you hear the beep. Continue listening when you have said your part.

MEDIATION

_____ / 14

A day trip to Heidelberg

Your school is planning a day trip to Heidelberg. Your exchange student from the USA doesn't understand everything your teacher says.

14 ***a)*** *Listen to your teacher's announcements and explain them to your exchange student in English. Then complete your answers in English. (3P)*

Your teacher ...
Student I didn't get all the details about tomorrow. Do we have to bring an alarm clock?

You No, you needn't bring _______________. But it's important that you arrive _______________________________.

15 ***b)*** *Now listen to more of your teacher's announcements. Help your friend in English. Stop the recording when you hear the beep. (11P)*

- Höre die Ansagen des Lehrers nur einmal an.
- Halte nach jedem Abschnitt die Tonaufnahme an und versuche, deinem Austauschpartner die Ansagen des Lehrers zu vermitteln.
- Vergleiche abschließend deine gesamte Lösung mit der Musterlösung.
- Wenn nötig, wiederhole die Aufgabe und ergänze deine Lösungen.

Your teacher ...
Student I understood that we're going to visit Heidelberg Castle. That's great. But what was that about the camera? And do we have to write something?

You We should bring our cameras _______________________________
_______________________________.

We need a pen and some paper for _______________________________
_______________________________.

Your teacher ...
Student What was that about three people? I didn't understand what the teacher said.

You In the afternoon we have free time in Heidelberg. We have to _______________
_______________________________.

Student And do we have to do anything special in our groups?

You No, we _______________________________.
Student And where do we meet after that?

You _______________________________.
Your teacher ...
Student We'll be back by 6 pm. Is there anything else that's important for me to know?

You Yes, _______________________________.

Klassenarbeit A

Gesamtpunktzahl ______ / 93 Note ______

LISTENING

______ / 11

16 CASA – Come and see Atlanta!

You are going to hear an announcement about Atlanta by the CASA travel agency[1]. Read the task and then listen to the announcement.

About CASA

While listening to the announcement, complete the sentences in 1–7 words.

1 CASA is an organization that offers ______________________________.

2 They have a lot of experience because they've been organizing these tours ______________________________.

3 If you only want to see the most important sights in Atlanta, you should book ______________________________.

4 If you have any questions while you are on the tour, ______________________________.

5 There are special guides for people ______________________________.

6 If you want to visit the King Center, ______________________________.

7 The Stone Mountain Tour offers something ______________________________.

8 Underground Atlanta has ______________________________.

9 If you book a personal tour, you just have to tell CASA what you want to see and ______________________________.

10 The tour will be by car if there are ______________________________.

11 If you like, the tour can start ______________________________.

[1] travel agency ['trævl 'eɪdʒənsi] *Reisebüro*

LANGUAGE

____/61

1 WORDS Martin Luther King Jr.

____/10

a) *Here is some information about Martin Luther King Jr. and the King Center. Find the missing words and fill them in. (9P)*

1 In the __________ of the King Center you can find out a great deal of information about Martin Luther King Jr.

2 Martin Luther King Jr. was a Baptist minister and one of the leaders of the American ______ ________ movement.

3 Martin Luther King Jr. led the Montgomery Bus ________ in 1955.

4 At that time blacks didn't have the same rights as whites – there was ____________ in the American South.

5 Martin Luther King Jr. fought for ______ rights for black people.

6 At that time African Americans and white Americans were kept ______.

7 In 1963 Martin Luther King Jr. became famous following the _____ on Washington where he made his speech 'I have a dream'.

8 He was killed five years later in 1968 – April 4th is the ____________ of his death.

9 A wide selection of books, DVDs and CDs is on _______ at the King Center.

b) *Can you make a word with the letters from the blue boxes? If not, look at the sentence below. It will help you. (1P)*

_ _ _ _ _ _ _ _ _ _ _

Martin Luther King Jr. asked people to ____________________ in non-violent actions.

2 WORDS At the King Center

____ / 13

*Complete the text below. Use **nouns** made from the **verbs** in the box.*
Be careful: some nouns have the same form as the verbs, others don't. You don't need all the words.

☞ Wenn du dir unsicher bist, bilde zunächst Nomen zu allen Verben im Kasten und mache dir ihre Bedeutung klar. Versuche dann, sie an den richtigen Stellen einzusetzen.

Beispiele:
(to) delay ▶ delay = Verspätung
(to) react ▶ reaction = Reaktion

arrive • cost • delay • fight • inform • introduce • live • protest • react • segregate • sort • support • talk • visit • volunteer

In their summer holidays Judy and Gareth went to Atlanta. On the second day after their ____________________, they went to the King Center to learn about the ____________________ of Martin Luther King Jr. They shared the ____________________ of the taxi to the museum, the Center itself was free. At the beginning of their ____________________ they were given an ____________________ to Martin Luther King's ____________________ against ____________________. They learned that ____________________ for his ideas is still important today. They were also told that there was a ____________________ on ____________________ work at the Center later, but as tourists they were not interested. They went to the picture gallery where they saw photos taken at the different ____________________ marches Martin Luther King organized. Next to the photos they found ____________________ on where they were taken. The last photo showed Martin Luther King just minutes before he was shot by James Earl Ray as a ____________________ to his speeches.

3 WORDS Verbs and nouns

____ / 25

***a)** Here is a list of words. Circle the ones which can be both **verbs** and **nouns**. (15P)*

bury cause change confuse copy cost cut dress elect enter fight
fill hand hike hope hug kiss move paint plant pray prevent
programme protest report sale scream smoke segregate separate show
solve sort support surprise stop sweat talk taste wave work

***b)** Choose five words that can be both **verbs** and **nouns** from **a)** and make sentences. Write one sentence where the word is used as a **verb** and one sentence where it is a **noun**. Use your exercise book. (10P)*

4 GRAMMAR At the station

___ /5

*In the picture you can see people at a station in Atlanta. Who is who? Make sentences with **defining relative clauses**.*

Defining relative clauses

Ein **defining relative clause** (bestimmender Relativsatz) gibt Informationen über ein Nomen, die zum Verständnis des Satzes notwendig sind. Ein solcher Relativsatz wird nie durch Kommas abgetrennt.
Eingeleitet werden diese Relativsätze mit den Relativpronomen

- **who** oder **that** für Personen und
- **which** oder **that** für Dinge.

Beispiele:
The station **which/that** is closest to the Georgia Aquarium is Peachtree Center Station.
The people **who/that** can be seen in this picture are waiting for the next train.

1 The man / drink coffee / have got two children

The man who is drinking coffee has got two children.

2 The woman / stand on platform / have her daughter with her.

___

3 The little girl / hug a bear / look pleased

___

4 The bike / block the information point / belong to one of the children

___

5 The girl / shout / be sad because she has missed the train

___

6 The poster / hang on the wall / be for the Georgia Aquarium

___

5 GRAMMAR A project on Martin Luther King Jr.

___/8

Relative clauses with 'which' to refer to a whole clause

Relativsätze können sich nicht nur auf vorhergehende Nomen, sondern auch auf ganze Sätze beziehen. Mit solchen Relativsätzen kommentiert man die Aussage im vorausgehenden Hauptsatz. Man verwendet hier immer das Relativpronomen **which** und trennt den Relativsatz mit einem Komma vom Hauptsatz ab.

Beispiel:
Helen likes studying modern history. Pete finds that rather strange.
Helen likes studying modern history, **which** Pete finds rather strange.

A high school class has done a project on Martin Luther King Jr. (MLK). Find out what they did and what happened.

a) *Match the sentences on the left with the correct sentences on the right. (3P)*

1 Not many people answered the students' questions.	a) They thought this was an interesting experience.
2 Tom had to ask people in the street what they knew about MLK.	b) That was very disappointing for them.
3 The teacher told the students they should always ask the ladies first when they interviewed a couple.	c) The teacher was very pleased about this.
4 At the library Tracy and Pharrell read some newspapers from 1968.	d) This terrified him.
5 Sophie enjoyed reading MLK's speeches.	e) The class found this very entertaining.
6 One group showed a video of their interviews.	f) That seemed a bit old-fashioned to them.

b) *Use the information from* ***a)*** *and make* ***relative sentences that refer to the whole sentence****. (5P)*

1 Not many people answered the students' questions, which was very disappointing for them.

2 ______________________________

3 ______________________________

4 ______________________________

____

5 ______________________________

____

6 ______________________________

____

MEDIATION

____ / 21

At the CASA travel agency

- Übersetze nicht wörtlich, sondern sinngemäß.
- Gib das Wesentliche wieder.
- Verwende kurze und einfache Sätze.
- Umschreibe unbekannte Wörter.

The Kurz family from Göttingen is on holiday in Georgia. Today they are visiting Atlanta and want to book a tour. They are in the CASA office. Their son Niklas helps his parents because their English is not very good. Write what Niklas says.

Frau Kurz Sagst du bitte der Dame, dass wir eine Tour für vier Personen mitmachen möchten.

Niklas ______________________________ (1P)

Lady Well, let's see. We've got different tours to choose from. What exactly would you like to see?

Niklas ______________________________ (2P)

Herr Kurz Na ja, auf jeden Fall die Innenstadt, finde ich.

Niklas ______________________________ (1P)

Lady Then I can offer you our Tour 21. You'll see all the sights in downtown Atlanta, you'll visit CNN and the World of Coca-Cola* and the tour ends at Underground Atlanta*.

Niklas ______________________________

____

______________________________ (4P)

Frau Kurz Was ist denn Underground Atlanta?

Niklas ______________________________ (1P)

Lady It's a large area below street level[1] with a great selection of shops, restaurants and cinemas. It's an ideal place to relax after the long day tour. You could also have dinner there.

Niklas ______________________________

____

______________________________ (4P)

Herr Kurz Mir gefällt die Tour. Niklas, frag bitte noch, wo und wann die Tour beginnt.

Niklas ______________________________ (2P)

Lady If you are staying in a hotel in Atlanta, we can pick you up there at 10.30 in the morning.

Niklas ______________________________

______________________________ (2P)

Frau Kurz Das ist ja wunderbar. Frag bitte, wieviel es für vier Personen kostet.

Niklas ______________________________ (1P)

Lady We have a special offer for families: it's $42 for the four of you. Would that be OK?

Niklas ______________________________ (2P)

Herr Kurz Dann buchen wir die Tour für morgen.

Niklas ______________________________ (1P)

* Eigennamen musst du nicht ins Deutsche übertragen.

[1] below street level [bɪˈləʊ striːt ˈlevl] *hier: unter der Erde*

Klassenarbeit B

Gesamtpunktzahl ohne Speaking ______ / 56 Note ______

Gesamtpunktzahl mit Speaking ______ / 77 Note ______

READING

______ / 21

Take Your Child To Work Day (TYCTWD)

Every year in April parents in the USA can take their children to work for the day. This day is called 'Take Your Child to Work Day' (TYCTWD) and lots of families and companies take part in it. Read the discussions in the web community about TYCTWD.

In two weeks' time it's "Take Your Child to Work Day" again, and my daughter (9 years old) wants to come to my office with me. I work for the mayor of a small town. Has anyone had any experience with TYCTWD? Is it a good thing? I'm not sure what I should do.
Any comments welcome.

Anne I 36 I Oneonta I 8th April I 10.00

Last year we had about 45 kids, aged 6–13 at our TV studio. They went on a tour of the building, learning about what we do, how we broadcast our programs and the way we get information from the different news agencies. As most children were too young to really participate in the real work of the TV studio, we thought up some fun things for them to do during the day. We organized a lot of activities, such as interviewing several people who work for us and meeting two directors in the conference room. We also thought of some games to keep the kids entertained, which were very successful. When they first arrived at 9.30 in the morning, we played a game to get to know each other. We had a word game with all the names of the people who work in our department[1], we had quizzes and activities that kept them moving around the building. By the end of the day most of the kids said they wanted to work in our TV studio when they grew up.
The day was a great success.

Sue I 51 I Iowa I 8th April I 11.02

One of the best days I spent while growing up was when I went to work with my dad for the first time on TYCTWD. I still remember every minute of the day. I felt very grown-up, as if I was already going to work. Of course I had a day off school so that was a good thing to start with! But being together with my dad at his office and being able to watch him at work was a great experience for me. He took me along to a couple of meetings, we had lunch together in the cafeteria and I helped him with a few things like taking messages, making photocopies and things like that. The day also motivated me to work harder at school. I can only say: TYCTWD is a good thing! Once I have children of my own I'll take them to my company too.

Terry I 25 I Philadelphia I 10th April I 19.00

→

[1] department [dɪˈpɑːtmənt] *Abteilung*

The idea of TYCTWD is to show your children what you do at work. It also helps your child to discover the link between what they learn at school and what they might do as a grown-up. In most companies there are special hands-on activities and workshops to show the children what the company does.
Before you take your daughter to your office, you should make sure that:
- she is old enough to understand what you do, as she might be disappointed if she can't really help you with your work,
- your place of work offers special activities and workshops for her and the other kids,
- she doesn't miss too many important lessons at school,
- she is interested in what you do.

If all this is true for you, then give her the chance to spend a day at your office.

Leona | 49 | Atlanta | 12th April | 00.36

1 Who's this?

____ / 12

Look at the following twelve sentences. Who are they about? Write the correct names in the gaps to complete the sentences. Be careful: four sentences aren't about anyone!

1 ______________ works at the mayor's office.

2 ______________ explains what TYCTWD can look like.

3 ______________ is looking for young people to work at her company.

4 ______________ thinks that TYCTWD is for young children only.

5 ______________ says that you need special activities for children on TYCTWD.

6 ______________ was given small jobs to do on TYCTWD.

7 ______________ hasn't forgotten when he was taken on TYCTWD.

8 ______________ is not sure if TYCTWD is a good idea.

9 ______________ gives some important points to think about before taking your child to work.

10 ______________ doesn't know when TYCTWD is.

11 ______________ talks about experiences with children in her company.

12 ______________ took her child to work last year.

2 About the web discussion

____ / 9

Read the discussion in the web community and answer the questions in 1–5 words. Use your exercise book.

1 What activities could the students take part in at Sue's company? *(three things)*

2 What did Terry do on his TYCTWD? *(three things)*

3 What should parents think about before their children take part in TYCTWD? *(three things)*

LANGUAGE

____ / 22

1 WORDS A new radio station

____ / 8

Look at this flyer which a new radio station has produced to attract listeners. Fill in the missing words. Be careful: sometimes you need more than one word.

Atlanta FM on 89.3 – your new local radio station with the best ____________________ for young and old. We want to ____________________ you about what's going on in Atlanta. Are you interested in the latest news from the city government or fascinating stories about everyday life in Atlanta?

Our reporters are always ____________________ when something happens!

We ____________________ news quicker than anybody else and we entertain you too.

So ____________________ your radio on! Here are some of next week's highlights:

Tuesday, 9 pm – A radio ____________________: Slavery – a family torn apart.

Thursday, 7 pm – We open our ____________________ and bring you the funniest sound clips you have ever heard.

Saturday, 10 am – From the event to the news – a documentary on how a ____________________ works.

2 WORDS Opposites

____ / 8

a) *Re-write the following sentences without changing their meanings. Use the opposite of the underlined adjectives. Write the sentences in your exercise book. (4P)*

1 The clothes she was wearing were not modern.

2 People who have expensive cars are usually not poor.

3 The streets were not very clean after the weekend.

4 Tours at the King Center are not boring.

b) *Look at the pictures and correct the sentences. Use the opposite of the underlined words. (4P)*

1 

Tom can see that his flight has a new arrival time. ____________________

2 

The novel was expensive. It only cost $3.99. ____________________

3 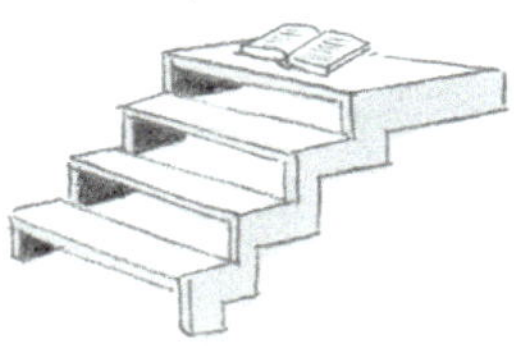

There is a book at the bottom of the stairs. ____________________

4 disadvantage The suffix in this word is 'dis'. ____________________

3 GRAMMAR Facts about Georgia

_____ /6

Look at the following sentences about Georgia. Use the information in brackets below to add a ***non-defining relative clause*** *to each sentence.*

1 Georgia was the last of the original thirteen colonies.

Georgia, which was founded in 1732, was the last of the original thirteen colonies.

2 Georgia was named after King George II of England.

____

3 Jimmy Carter was born in Georgia.

____

4 Augusta is the second largest city in Georgia.

____

5 Julia Roberts comes from Atlanta.

____

6 Georgia's population had the fastest growing Asian population in the US in the 1990s.

____

7 The most famous version of the song 'Georgia on my mind' is by Ray Charles.

____

a) (which was founded in 1732)
b) (whose best known film is 'Pretty Woman')
c) (which is also known as the 'Peach[1] State')
d) (which is mainly[2] white)
e) (who was born in Albany, Georgia)
f) (which is on the Savannah River)
g) (who was the 39th President of the USA)

Non-defining relative clauses

Non-defining relative clauses geben Zusatzinformationen, die für das Verständnis des Satzes nicht unbedingt notwendig sind. Man kann in diesen Relativsätzen nur die Relativpronomen **who, which** und **whose** verwenden. Die nicht bestimmenden Relativsätze werden mit Kommas vom Hauptsatz abgetrennt.

[1] peach [piːtʃ] *Pfirsich* [2] mainly ['meɪnli] *hauptsächlich*

SPEAKING

____ / 21

17 Eric's day at the restaurant

Lots of students in class 8 at a high school in Atlanta took part in TYCTWD. Today they're reporting about their day. Listen to Eric.

a cook

Höre dir Erics Vortrag noch einmal an und notiere dir nützliche Redewendungen. Sie helfen dir, wenn du in **Now you** selbst über deine Arbeitserfahrungen sprichst.

Now you

Now report about your experience. Speak about some work experience[1] you have done or a Girls'/Boys' Day you took part in. Choose a job from the pictures below or talk about another job of your choice.

Give information on
- what kind of work experience you did, (1P)
- where you went, (1P)
- when your day started and ended, (1P)
- what you saw and did during the day (at least four things*), (8P)
- what you liked or didn't like (at least three things*). (6P)

End your talk with your opinion about the day and the job. (4P)

Gliedere deinen Vortrag mit Hilfe von **linking words** (z. B. **first**, **after that**, ...).

firefighters

doctors

architects

a make up artist

[1] work experience [ˈwɜːk ɪkspɪəriəns] *Praktikum*

* Jedes zusätzliche Detail erhöht die Punktzahl um 2 Punkte.

WRITING

___/13

Your opinion about TYCTWD

You have searched the internet and read the discussion about TYCTWD in the web community. Write your own entry. What do you think about TYCTWD? Use the ideas below. Write about 150 words.

- Write who you are and where you're writing from. (2P)
- How you know about TYCTWD. (1P)
- Write whether activities like TYCTWD exist in Germany too. (2P)
- Give your opinion about TYCTWD. (2P)
- Write whether TYCTWD should be introduced in Germany or not and give two reasons. (2P)
- Which job would you like to experience for one day and why? (2P)
- What would you do on that day? (1P)
- Write a suitable[1] ending. (1P)

[1] suitable ['suːtəbl] *passend*

Kompetenztest

Gesamtpunktzahl ohne Speaking ______ / 71	Note ______
Gesamtpunktzahl mit Speaking ______ / 86	Note ______

TEIL 1: LISTENING

______ / 13

14 Radio and TV in your lives – a radio programme

Listen to the radio programme about what British people like about radio and TV programmes. While you are listening, complete the table below. Tick the correct box or write 1 to 3 words if there is a question word. There is an example at the beginning (Emily). Listen to the recording only once. Take 20 seconds at the end of the recording to check your answers. Now take 30 seconds to look at the task.

	In the morning			During the day		In the evening	
	Radio	TV	Nothing	Radio	TV	Radio	TV
Emily	✔			✔			
				When? in the afternoon		What? ______	What? ______
Steve							
				When? ______		What? ______	What? ______
Anne							
				When? ______		What? ______	What? ______

TEIL 2: SPEAKING

______ / 15

Me, my day, radio and TV

While you are staying in Southampton, England you are listening to the radio programme Teatime. The programme's presenter has asked listeners to tell him when they listen to the radio and when they watch TV during the day. He also wants to find out about listeners' favourite programmes.

Take ten minutes to prepare your call. Look at the pictures and the task. You can make notes.

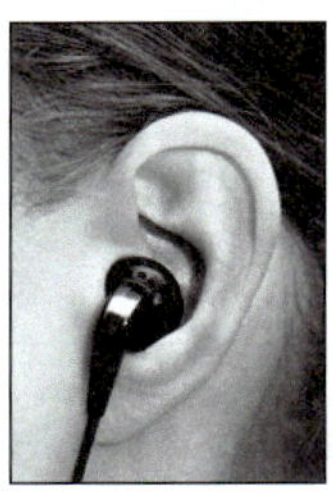

Ring up and tell them ...
- who you are and where you are calling from.
- which programmes you listen to or watch in Germany ...
  - in the morning before you leave the house,
  - in the afternoon,
  - in the evening.

Give a reason why you listen to or watch one of the programmes.

TEIL 3: MEDIATION

___/16

Your class is planning a school trip to the south-west of England. In groups you are preparing activities to do during your stay. You and your group are preparing a visit to Southwest Radio and TV, a local radio and TV station.

Read the information about tours at Southwest Radio and TV.

Southwest Radio and TV

A visit to the studios

Come and find out what goes on inside Southwest Radio and TV, your regional centre for radio and TV!
Your tour guide will give you an insight into our many programmes and he is ready to answer all your questions. Visitors will have the chance to see a real TV studio. You'll also pop into the radio studios and hear how radio programmes are produced.

You'll not only learn how television and radio programmes are made, you'll also have the chance to visit our interactive studio. Have a go at presenting the weather or be a star in your very own radio drama, complete with sound effects!

Southwest Radio and TV is a working building so no two tours are the same, but they will always be informative, interesting and fun.

Our tours

★ take about one hour and 45 minutes and involve a certain amount of walking and standing.

★ take place on Tuesdays at 10.00 am and 3.15 pm (plus Wednesdays and Saturdays from 14 July).

★ are open to anyone aged 10 years and over. A group tour booked for under-16s must have at least two accompanying adults.

★ take a maximum of 25 people on each tour.

★ have to be pre-booked.

★ are free of charge.

You may take photos in the studios as advised by our tour guides, but some of the working areas are restricted. Video cameras are not permitted on the tours except in our Interactive Studio.

Contact us on 0044-1752-395953 or send an e-mail to visit@southwestradio.co.uk

Your classmates are asking you a lot of questions about the tour. Answer the questions in German. Use full sentences.

1 Ist es eine geführte Tour? Und was können wir bei der Führung alles sehen? *(3 Dinge)* (4P)

____

____

____

2 Kann man da auch selbst etwas machen und wenn ja, was? *(2 Dinge)* (2P)

____

____

____

3 Wie lange dauert die Tour?

____

4 Um wie viel Uhr beginnen die Touren?

____

____

5 Wie ist es mit der Gruppengröße?

____

6 Gibt es sonst Dinge, die wir als Schulklasse beachten müssen?

____

____

7 Darf man überall fotografieren und auch Videos drehen?

____

____

8 Muss man sich da anmelden und wie viel kostet der Besuch?

____

TEIL 4: READING

____/12

The British and their soap operas

Read the text taken from a language magazine for students carefully. Then answer the questions below.

In Britain some of the most popular programmes on television are soap operas or soaps. Soaps are dramas usually shown in half hour episodes, three, four and sometimes five times a week. The most popular soaps in Britain are *Coronation Street* (known as *Corrie* by its fans) and *EastEnders*, although there are many more as well. Both *Coronation Street* and *EastEnders* have been running for a long time – in fact in December 2010 it was *Coronation Street's* 50th birthday. ITV, the TV channel which produces *Corrie*, showed a special live episode and a documentary about the history of the soap.

Coronation Street and *EastEnders* tell stories of the everyday lives of families living in Manchester and the East End of London. In both programmes community life often takes place in the local pub, the Rovers Return and the Queen Vic. As in other soap operas, stories with different characters are shown over many episodes, and there are always different stories running at the same time. Some of the characters have been in the shows for many years. The actors have become famous playing their roles, and the characters are loved by fans.

In British soaps the stories are unglamorous and show family life, friendship and conflicts. Over the years, *Coronation Street* and *EastEnders* have also included stories about difficult problems like AIDS, drugs, violence and alcoholism. In this way, soap operas have helped to change the way people think about important topics, although some stories have upset people. But not all the stories are so serious! There are also comedy storylines, which viewers like a lot too.

Soap operas play a very special role in British culture. Did you know that the very first British soap was made for the radio and is still being produced by the BBC today? The Archers started in 1951 and is still listened to by over 5 million people.

The very first TV soap operas were shown during the daytime and were mostly watched by housewives. The name soap opera comes from the fact that the programmes were often produced and supported by soap companies who wanted the viewers to buy their products, like washing powder. These days soaps in Britain are shown at prime time and have big audiences – both *Coronation Street* and *EastEnders* often have 10 million viewers.

Answer the questions. Write one to five key words only. Number 1 has been done for you as an example.

1 What are soap operas? dramas, half hour episodes

2 What are the most famous soaps on British TV? ______________________________

3 Where do the characters in these soap operas live? ______________________________

4 What are these soaps about? ______________________________

5 Who watched the soaps when they first started? ______________________________

6 What is the name of the first ever British soap? Can you watch it on television?

____

7 What did companies selling washing powder have to do with soap operas?

____

TEIL 5: WORDS

____/12

The British and their soap operas

a) *Find the word in the text for ... (5P)*

1 the different sections of a soap opera shown three, four or five times a week: ____________________

2 people who act in films, theatre or on television: ____________________

3 people who watch TV: ____________________

4 (to) make someone sad or angry: ____________________

b) *These words are from the text. Find one opposite for each word:*

1 many (line 4): ____________________

2 different (line 9): ____________________

3 serious (line 17): ____________________

4 daytime (line 22): ____________________

c) *Circle the word that doesn't fit in the group. There is an example at the beginning (1).*

1 often, sometimes, (never) usually

2 produce, sell, buy, watch

3 product, pub, company, shop

4 channel, film, programme, newspaper

5 soap, support, water, shower

TEIL 6: WRITING

___ / 15

An article for the school magazine

Your American friend is the editor of a school magazine. He has asked some students to write about their favourite films.

Write a short text of about 100 words about one of your favourite films.

Write about ...
- the name of the film and what it is about,
- when and where you saw it,
- the characters in the film,
- why you liked the film.

How to do well in a test

Countdown zum Testerfolg

Ein Test ist angekündigt? Kein Grund zur Panik. Wichtig ist, dass du weißt, worauf du dich vorbereiten musst. Im Zweifelsfall frag deine Lehrerin oder deinen Lehrer. Der Countdown kann beginnen!

Eine Woche vor dem Test

1 Lies noch einmal die **Texte** der zuletzt durchgenommenen Unit (A-Section und Text, eventuell auch das Background File). Fasse mündlich oder schriftlich zusammen, worum es ging.

2 Wiederhole den **Wortschatz** der Unit mit Hilfe des *Vocabulary* oder des *Wordmaster*. Schreibe dir die Wörter und Wortverbindungen, die du immer wieder vergisst, auf ein Blatt Papier. Eine Mindmap oder ein Wortfeld helfen beim Behalten.

3 Geh auch noch mal die neue **Grammatik** durch. Aufgaben zur Selbstüberprüfung und zum Üben findest du im *Practice*-Teil, auf der Seite „How am I doing?", im *Grammar File* (S. 172–189), in deinem *Workbook* und im *e-Workbook*.

Zwei Tage vor dem Test

1 Wiederhole den **Wortschatz**. Manche Wörter sitzen noch nicht? Schreibe einen kurzen Text, in dem du sie verwendest.

2 Lies die **Texte** ein weiteres Mal.

3 Erkläre einem Freund oder einer Freundin die neue **Grammatik**. Das klappt nicht richtig? Dann lies nochmal im *Grammar File* nach.

Am Abend vor dem Test

1 Entspanne dich. Du kannst lesen, dich in die Badewanne legen, Musik hören, fernsehen, ...

2 Geh zur gewohnten Zeit ins Bett.

Am Morgen des Tests

1 Steh rechtzeitig auf, damit du nicht hetzen musst.

2 Lies irgendetwas „zum Aufwärmen", aber schau nicht mehr in dein Schülerbuch.

Während des Tests

1 Denk daran: Du hast dich gut vorbereitet. Es gibt keinen Grund, nervös zu sein.

2 Konzentriere dich auf den Test, lass dich nicht ablenken.

3 Lies dir die Aufgaben genau durch. Dann löse zuerst die Aufgaben, die dir einfach scheinen. Wende dich erst danach den schwereren Aufgaben zu.

4 Aufgaben, die du bearbeitet hast, hakst du ab. So siehst du, wie du vorankommst, und behältst den Überblick.

5 Schau ab und zu auf die Uhr. Du solltest dir für den Schluss noch etwas Zeit einplanen, um deine Antworten noch einmal durchzulesen und wenn nötig zu korrigieren.